DEALING WITH THE SUBCONSCIOUS MIND

"This book is the most precious and meaningful gift for our grandparents and parents, because the most important matters for elders are good health and mental lucidity until their final moment."

"The elderly in the new generation should not live for the purposes of eating, sleeping, enjoying their life or waiting for the death to come. Instead, they should practice the True Buddha Dharma in order to save themselves, save people and others being."

- Bhiksu Thich Thanh Thien -

On behalf of many Buddhist practitioners, we'd like to respectfully express our utmost gratitude to Arhat Thich Thong Lac, whose revelation of True Buddha Dharma has saved us from ignorance and our addiction to heretical beliefs and, furthermore, has given us the ability to believe in ourselves again to take on the challenging journey of self-rescue and self-conquest to finally liberate ourselves from all sufferings.

BHIKSU THICH THANH THIEN

DEALING WITH
THE SUBCONSCIOUS MIND

Translator: ĐÀI TIẾNG NÓI CHÁNH PHẬT PHÁP
(Youtube)

Albert Einstein once declared:

"The religion of the future will be a cosmic religion. It should transcend a person God and avoid dogmas and theology. Covering both the natural and the spiritual, it should be based on a religious sense, arising from the experience of all things, natural and spiritual, as a meaningful unity. If there is any religion that would cope with modern scientific needs, it would be Buddhism."

THE BRIEF HISTORY OF SHAKYAMUNI BUDDHA

It is said in many documents that Shakyamuni Buddha became a monk due to his compassion for suffering beings, but through meditation, my Master and I realized this is not to be exact. Shakyamuni Buddha was born in around 624 BC in India with the name Siddhartha, and was a prince, the only son of King Suddhodana. At age 20, the prince was trained to be a king, but as he was going sightseeing outside of the castle, he saw the suffering of all living beings in the way of birth/life, aging, sickness, and death. It is true that he realized the suffering of all, but what he could not understand was why every human and creature had to undergo the rule of living and death; and to find the answer, he had to leave the castle and become a monk. However, according to the circumstances and tradition of that era, it was a must for him to get married, give birth to an heir to fulfill his duties before leaving. On the night when his wife gave birth to a son, he immediately left the castle and everything behind with the only clothes on his body to look for the answers to life. Unlike the thoughts of other ordinary people, Siddharta decided to become a monk and find the answers to life to escape from his own suffering.

Becoming a monk, he changed his name to Gotama and started living a life of an ascetic. He kept himself with little or no food; sometimes he only had a few beans and left himself starving until he fainted. Luckily, thanks to a girl who passed by and gave him some goat's milk to help him and he was revived. Since then, he understood that either abstaining from food or indulging himself with lots of food was wrong, so he decided to have one meal a day which was just enough to sustain his body to patiently go on with his quest. In other words, he ate to live for the purpose of his journey, not live to eat and enjoy his life.

He kept striving through the six different practice methods from six different masters. Each of the method he completed, he achieved a level higher than the masters. At this level, he recognized that both he and his masters were not practicing the correct way to attain enlightenment to free themselves from birth, aging, sickness and death, even their human nature of greed, hatred and delusions had not yet left them; they might have supernatural powers that ordinary people could not achieve but that was not enlightenment.

As a result, up to the sixth method, having honorably nominated to become a master of each method because of having reached the final stage of The Four Stages of Great Awakening acquired through subconsciousness practices, which is the state of Neither Subconsciousness nor Non-subconsciousness, he still refused. He decided to find the answer by himself and announced that he would abandon those four stages like abandoning a tattered shoe – those words shocked every monk as if they had been struck on the head by a hammer!

Having meditated on his own for many days and still not yet attained Enlightenment, he suddenly remembered the time when he was ten years old, as he was at a tree stump waiting for his father to attend a royal rite, he started meditating and found himself entering into a kind of unknown realm of senses that gave him a strange feeling. Thus he decided to recall the status he had before. He sat under another tree called Bodhi tree which is located in Bodhi Gaya, India where he attained enlightenment (*Bodhi means enlightenment)*. As an enlightened one, he realized that there were two types of meditation, such as:

1. The Four Stages of Enlightenment acquired through practicing meditation consciously (which are The Four Noble Meditational States or The Four Dhyanas), including:

- Stream-enterer (free from identity view, attachment to heresy, and doubts about the teachings).

- One-returner (has greatly attenuated sensorial desires and ill will).

- Non-returner (free from sensorial desires and ill will) - Arhat (free from rebirth cycle, attains knowledge of the Truths, and reaches to the top of wisdom, i.e. the Threefold Knowledge).

2. The Four Stages of Great Awakening acquired through subconsciousness practices, which is also a type of meditational concentration or awakening but still under the sway of birth, aging, sickness and death, and the person who acquires this still has their own casual personalities like all humans. The Four Stages include:

- Realm of boundless space.

- Realm of boundless consciousness.

- Realm of nothingness.

- Realm of Neither Subconsciousness nor Non-subconsciousness.

As an enlightened one, He, the Buddha, found the answer to his lifelong question: there are life and death because life is impermanent and our karma - actions of the body and mind from our previous lives - defines who we are today; whether we are human or animal, rich or poor, live a sinful or virtuous life; and all our actions in this life cause things to happen in the following lives. It is quite fortunate and precious to be a human, and it would be such a waste if we used our physical body ineffectively. The Buddha called that impermanence "Suffering" and established *The Four Truths revolved around Suffering,* also known as *The Four Noble Truths,* in order to help people practice and liberate from birth/life, aging, sickness and death.

Buddha brought *The Four Noble Truths* to all human beings in the way of respecting their views, choices and abilities. He never forced anyone to practice and never held anyone back if they wanted to give up, which means he did not try to persuade or save anyone who did not want to be saved. He merely taught those who choose to escape from their suffering. And finally, he successfully introduced thousands of Arhats to the world who began their practice with *The Four Noble Truths*. Many Arhats, many methods, but they had the same purpose, which is to attain enlightenment. Since the Buddha did not leave any written teachings, the Arhats mentally recalled and gathered all of His teachings into a collection called the Nikaya after He abandoned his earthly body.

The Buddha understood that everyone suffers, that is the reason why he disseminated his teachings, but he could not help people if they did not agree with *The Four Noble Truths* or weren't aware of helping themselves. From the beginning, Siddharta became a monk for himself, for his questions and for his own freedom, not for the sake of others. But sadly, after he was gone, people misled history and created misunderstandings among Buddhist practitioners with stories of how the Buddha became a monk because of them and that he became god-like with magical powers that can save their lives when He heard their prayers.

Hence, Buddhists nowadays show their gratitude toward Him by worshiping, donating food, assets and properties to temples and monks. This brought a backward mindset and has inadvertently ruined the pure and silent lives of today's monks, turned them into greedy and unethical people.

THE ONE AND ONLY SHAKYAMUNI

History has proven that Shakyamuni Buddha had entered six different paths before discovering his own way. It is evident that the Buddha was the master of Himself and that His attainment was under no guidance of any master. This means if there were already thousands of other Buddhas before Shakyamuni, it was not necessary for him to struggle through six other paths as he could have just used his royal privilege to seek out for the right master. Suppose there were really thousands of Buddhas from hundreds of years before Shakyamuni was born, at least one of them should have been destined to stay, obtained pupils and helped them attain their Enlightenment, then one or more of them would be able to continue to spread Buddhism until the existence of Shakyamuni.

Obviously, if that hypothesis were true, Buddhism must have been very popular in the ancient world. But the archeological evidence has proven to us that in such period, Buddhism had not existed in any country, and India was still under the control of Hinduism. Some people may argue it was because Siddharta did not know the existence of other Buddhas but he realized it after having attained enlightenment. So if He did really realize it, why were there no written stories of Him in the Nikaya visiting Amitabha, Matreya or other Buddhas to obtain other practicing experience for His pupils to learn from? Out of the great Arhats, Ananda had an extraordinary memory that could never have missed such important information when composing the Nikayas.

What is more, before giving his first Dharma talks, Shakyamuni Buddha had firmly announced that:

"For the first time in ever

There is only me

In this universe

That has overcome birth, aging, sickness and death"

As we can see, if there were a thousand Buddhas of the previous generation, this announcement would have been considered as an arrogant, foolish remark, and reflected an insignificant behavior of a person who did not deserve to be honoured. After enlightenment, Master Thich Thong Lac indicated that beside precious teachings, the Buddha has left both enlightened and unenlightened pupils. The poor unenlightened were like orphans when it came to follow the Nikayas' teachings without any master to guide them, give them motivation, or to alleviate some hardship during their practices. After the last Arhat, Ananda, left the world, the rest of the Buddha's pupils had no choice but to flee India because of their undignified manner and failure in upholding the moral principles. The Indian people had lost trust in these Buddhist monks, thus reversed their faith back to Hinduism. These monks ever since wandered everywhere to the neighboring countries, including China.

Being in China means those unenlightened monks had to respect its culture, customs and societal rules which, at the time, rested heavily upon the worship of many powerful deities in a way so that the Jade Emperor's and the almighty God's powers would be firmly consolidated and outspreaded. Buddhism therefore had to be altered so that it could fit in with the worship of Chinese people towards Mother Goddess, Thunder God and many others, because it was impossible to go on living as beggars like what the Buddha did (to survive) while the Chinese knew nothing about Buddhism.

As a result, Avalokitesvara was created as a loving mother, Amitabha was created as a God for the people to bow down to and appeal for. These creations had been mixed with the Buddha's original teachings by keeping *The Four Noble Truths* intact, but escaping from suffering depended on the compassion of Amitabha, which means prayers and offerings replaced the constant practice that strictly follows hundreds of precepts.

Accordingly, Buddhism became miraculous, superstitious, unscientific, and unethical for treating illness not by medicine but by prayers, earning not by laboring but by worshiping, and redemption not by laws but by sutra chanting. However, there is a strong belief that modern people today are not easy to be fooled like naive ancient people.

Today, it still is a sad reality to see small Shakyamuni statues in the main hall of many temples as a form's sake while marvelous, colossal statues of Amitabha, Avalokitesvara, Mahasthamaprapta are placed on majestic mountains; and in mentioning Buddhism, people would say "Namo Amitabha" as a habit. Indeed, Buddhism nowadays is merely a religion of which people take advantages to attract tourists, instead of being a noble path towards freedom from suffering. This fact is a heartache for those who resolve to abandon this impermanent world like us.

SHARINGS OF A PRACTITIONER TO BHIKSU THANH THIEN

Kim Ngọc

14:16, Tuesday, May 7, 2019

Dear Master,

I had read this book of yours online before your website's Admin sent me the paper copy. After reading the book, I felt that you provided me with a clear, detailed roadmap (for practicing the True Buddha Dharma) toward liberation. My dear Master, it is truly wonderful, simple, and neat. To be honest, I have listened to teachings of Venerable Thich

Thong Lac and of yourself many times but I could not systemize them into my own practice.

Now that I have read your book, I can clearly see the road toward liberation. I comfortably and gracefully execute each of your (practicing) lessons and put the statements on wise attention that you created - to tame the mind - to good use. Particularly, your method of long-distance walking meditation has brought me additional fortitude, joy, and enthusiasm in practicing the True Buddha Dharma. Now that Venerable Thich Thong Lac have reinstated the Dharma and you have further explained his teachings in clear and simple manners, it really is a great blessing for me to have a chance to practice the True Buddha Dharma for the sake of my liberation.

Dear Master, I am not the only one who has these sentiments. My peer practitioners are also extremely happy with your book.

Although videos of Venerable Thich Thong Lac's teachings are abundantly available online and all of them are useful, we are, however, unable to systematize those teachings into a suitable, organized protocol for each of us, because most of us practitioners have fallen into the state of mind suppression. Maybe our fundamentals of True Buddha Dharma are too shallow to comprehend the Venerable's teachings. Upon reading your book, I now can further understand the Venerable's teachings. We the ignorants are very lucky to have met you.

On behalf of practitioners, I would like to humbly send you our sincere gratitude.

GOOD WINE NEEDS NO BUSH!

THE AUTHOR'S FOREWORD

The buddha's method of critical thinking and commanding on wise attention is truly wonderful!

When Venerable Thich Thong Lac taught Bhiksu Thanh Thien about the method of critical thinking and commanding on wise attention, the Bhiksu was very confused at the time and did not know what to do with the method. Simultaneously, the Venerable taught the Bhiksu about the five Aggregates which made the Bhiksu even more confused about what he must do and how to practice the Dharma.

1) First off, Bhiksu Thanh Thien thought a lot about the five aggregates: "Indeed, this is the most important and critical knowledge for practitioners, because without knowing about ourselves, we would not have even the slightest idea of the why, the what, and the how of the Dharma practices. By thoroughly understanding that we have the five aggregates, particularly the subconscious mind, a flattering servant who constantly incites, lures, and feeds us with temptations and urges for sensorial gratification, can we start seeing that our life is drowning in depravations and in endless suffering of birth/life, old age, sickness, and death. Although our conscious mind tries to prevent and advise us to stay away from depravation, it is too weak to help us in the fight against our desires! That's why we practice the True Buddha Dharma to rescue ourselves from THE TORMENTS OF THE DISEASE. We need

to defeat our own subconscious mind which keeps inciting, luring, and driving us into desires and depravations, so that we can liberate our life from sufferings.

2) The real challenge here is how to fight to achieve self-rescue and self-defeat, and to overcome sufferings?

3) Bhiksu Thanh Thien found out that in order to achieve self-rescue and self-defeat and to overcome sufferings, we must tame the HEART because its sick obsession to desires have deeply rooted in our HEART and therefore the inclination to lure us into evil deeds and depravations.

4) The Buddha taught us the method of critical thinking and commanding on wise attention in order to tame the Heart. Bhiksu Thanh Thien thinks that we should deploy short sentences - using consciousness- to send commands to the (subconscious) Mind

so that it becomes familiar with them. Once the mind got used to the commands, it would lead our heart into realizing the wise attention that we want to cultivate!

5) Bhiksu Thanh Thien has experimented:

(1) On practicing vegetarianism: To be honest, Bhiksu Thanh Thien really wanted to practice vegetarianism but he had failed. Every time he had a vegetarian meal, even though the foods were very well made, it was impossible for Bhiksu Thanh Thien to bear through the meal. He felt as if he was tortured. He felt unsettled, quick to get hungry and extremely irritated. But with respect for his mother, Bhiksu Thanh Thien practiced vegetarian on the full moon and new moon days each month. Though, during those two days, he anxiously stayed up until midnight – the Buddha's bedtime. When the clock ticked 12am, he felt so liberated. He immediately

ran outside to buy a piece of *pha lau* (a kind of pork soup) from a Chinese street food shop at the nearby crossroad and ate it right away. Oh God, it felt so good, so enjoyable. After his mother died, he quitted vegetarianism altogether. Instead, he continuously partied, consumed alcohol, and become a severe alcoholic. Each day he took at least 48 cans of beer or a bottle of strong brandy.

It was like a miracle that after his pledge to take refuge in Buddha Dharma with the Venerable, Bhiksu Thanh Thien decided to become a vegetarian. He casually talked to himself repeatedly, for fun: "I should be a vegetarian. Eating animal flesh is too savage! Living beings also want to live, just like I do. Others can practice vegetarianism, so can I." He kept repeating the statements for 03 months. One day, he entered a restaurant without noticing that it was a full-moon day and that it was a vegetarian restaurant.

Because he was hungry, he ordered a random vegetarian dish. Unexpectedly, the food tasted so good and Bhiksu Thanh Thien did not feel any anxiety or irritation throughout that day. What was even more extraordinary is that when his relative served him a fuming savory bowl of beef noodles in the next morning, he did not have any appetite for it. Instead, he bought a portion of steamed sticky rice for breakfast. He took on vegetarianism with ease and peace ever since.

He found out that: because he repeated the statements constantly and persistently with a casual manner, the mind got used to the commands and became fond of them. As a result, beyond all expectations, he successfully switched to vegetarianism with ease for good.

(2) Making hay while the sun shines! With astounding victory, Bhiksu Thanh Thien decided to proceed with alcohol rehabilitation.

He thought to himself that how can he practice Buddha Dharma if he couldn't even quit drinking? So he cultivated that thought by repeating the command: (IF) I WANT TO PRACTICE BUDDHA DHARMA, I MUST QUIT ALCOHOLISM. He casually repeated the statement for over 03 months. Then during a party, while accompanied by sexy beautiful women, his friends were busy drinking and savoring animal flesh, Bhiksu Thanh Thien refused to drink. WOW! It felt amazing, beyond Bhiksu Thanh Thien's expectations. He successfully quitted alcoholism. He felt so light as if he was flying above clouds! He was so happy because he has successfully overcome alcoholism, the addiction that had tortured him for over 40 years. Wow! It was so delightful! So fascinating! The command on wise attention was indeed magical and amazing! Once the mind is familiar with the commanding statements, we can execute and achieve it! It is marvelous! With proper application of the Buddha's teaching, we would gradually imbue the wisdom (by repeating wise statements) into the mind. Once the wise attention is fully cultivated, we can easily execute it! How wonderful that is! He felt such a delightful and transcending rapture!

(3) Step by step, Bhiksu Thanh Thien reduced the number of meals until he can take only one meal per day in peace, and increased the time of practicing sitting in lotus position from 02 minutes to 05 minutes, and to the whole day without suffering any pain or irritation. One practice after another, he could proceed with comfort and peace.

(4) It is very important that Bhiksu Thanh Thien effectively combines the method of critical thinking on wise attention and the method of GRADUAL PROGRESS, so that the

mind gradually gets used to practices without rush. When a (wise) notion is embedded into the mind and when our heart becomes familiar with it and likes it, then it is the heart that drives us to execute and to live in that notion - a success beyond our expectations.

Bhiksu Thanh Thien

PREFACE

Ladies and gentlemen, if anyone among us has raised questions, such as "who am I?", "what is the meaning of this life?", he or she must have been very pleased to get to know the real Buddha's teaching. That is because Buddha Dharma guides us to clearly recognize our true human nature, the whole reason why we are present in this world and why we undergo the sufferings of Birth/Life, Old, Sickness, and Death. And most fantastically, the Buddha showed us methods and practices to overcome these four sufferings. However, the Buddha has gone for such a long time. There remains only the Nikaya Scriptures in which Arhats recorded the original Buddha

Teachings for their practices, which are really difficult for us to understand and follow.

Fortunately, Venerable Thich Thong Lac, an Enlightened One mastering birth, old, sickness and death like the Buddha, presents in the current age. It is enormously special and precious that an Arhat appears after more than 2,500 years! His Excellency has worked heartfully and diligently to provide opportunities for us to access the Correct Doctrines of the Buddha and furthermore to understand the Buddha Teachings. Sincerely grateful to the Venerable!

Even more fortunately, we have Bhiksu Thich Thanh Thien, the Venerable's disciple, who after successfully practicing the Venerable's teachings has voluntarily written them into sermons that are detailed, easy to understand, scientific and realistic practices, so that interested individuals could practice

Buddha Dharma properly. The book in your hands "Dealing With The Subconscious Mind" starts with lessons, revolving around the subconscious mind, which records precious practice experiences that Bhiksu Thanh Thien underwent and attained. The book also instructs practitioners on how to gradually get used to and start the Buddha Dharma practices properly. Because of that, we at the Voice of Correct Buddha Dharma are rapidly mobilizing resources to print the book and today happily introduce the book to you. We hope that this book will become a go-to book for your practice, so that each of you gradually study, practice and start the first steps in your quest to the Buddha land.

ANNOUNCEMENT

Greetings,

Bhiksu Thich Thanh Thien, up to this point, has three books (to be published):

1. DEALING WITH THE SUBCONSCIOUS MIND, a practicing guide from start to the attainment of the Truths.

2. SERMONS OF THE TRUE DHAMMA, that help practitioners in gaining a clear and correct understanding of the Shakyamuni Buddha's teaching.

3. PRACTITIONERS' DHAMMA INQUIRIES, shared helpful experiences in practicing the True Dhamma.

These are the three most valuable books to the progressive minds. They help people to comprehend correctly the Buddha's teaching which was unfortunately engulfed by heretical dogma for over the past 2550 years. Now that the True Dhamma has been resurrected and brought back to light by Arhat Thich Thong Lac, His teaching once again uplifts and illuminates many suffering souls around the world. And Bhiksu Thanh Thien furthermore expounds the Dhamma in much simple terms that anyone can understand.

This series of books are essential for the elderly of the new era, because the elderly shouldn't just be complacent and self-indulgent while on the other hand hopelessly suffer with illnesses and wait for their passing, and burden their children. Such mentality is antiquated! Instead, they need to wisely use their leisure time into practicing the Dhamma so that they can save themselves, save others, and save sentient beings. Nothing is more precious, to the elderly, than good health. These three books provide just the perfect answers to all of the elderly's concerns.

Thich Tu Duc

The Voice of the True Buddha Dharma

WHY DID VENERABLE THICH THONG LAC SAY THAT RECITING AMITABHA WOULD PARALYZE WISDOM?

Bhiksu Thanh Thien explained that reciting anything would paralyze wisdom, including reciting the Great Name of Shakyamuni Buddha.

Firstly, Science, Ministry of Education, and those who have been seeking the Path of Righteousness, let's be sincerely grateful to Arhat Thich Thong Lac who has clearly enlightened us on the Buddha's teachings of the five aggregates so that we can finally understand what we are truly made of.

It is precious to be human, a sapient being! Though being sapient, we do not clearly understand ourselves. Because we do not clearly understand ourselves, we blindly dive in vice and debauchery like moths to flame. So, we are just like the disgusting animals, aren't we?

The insight of the five aggregates is the most precious thing that Venerable Thong Lac has bestowed on everybody. Thanks to this clear understanding of Ourselves, we can then tirelessly take on the fight against each and every temptation that our Subconscious Mind strikes with and progress further into our liberating quest from suffering.

1- What is the subconscious mind?

(1) The Buddha taught that humans are made of five aggregates, or processes: Consciousness, Sensation, Subconsciousness,

Operating Mechanism, and Enlightening Consciousness (or Consciousness of the Heart).

Consciousness: includes many functions, including (short term) memory. Conscious Mind is temporarily called Trustworthy Servant by Bhiksu Thanh Thien for a better understanding. Conscious Mind works in limited space and time. Particularly, only when humans reach adult age can Conscious Mind start operating and operates very slowly.

Sensation: is a capacity of absorbing and expressing feelings, including pleasure, joy, sadness, suffering, salt, sweetness, bitterness, chilliness, warmth, softness, and pain. Sensation itself, however, does not have Awareness; therefore it doesn't have its own *mind*.

Subconsciousness: is a function of long-term habitual memory without any discernment. Subconscious Mind, which

Bhiksu Thanh Thien temporarily called Flattering Servant, for an easier-to-grasp concept. Subconscious Mind operates beyond space and time, and it starts working right from birth, thus it works very actively and strongly.

Operating Mechanism: is a servant function which works by directions. It operates in the absence of Awareness, thus it doesn't have a *mind* of its own.

Enlightening Consciousness: is dormant in humans and can only be activated through the attainment of consciousness meditations. Enlightening consciousness operates beyond space and time. Enlightening consciousness helps us to leave this world at will, without pain or difficulties, (temporarily called Legal Suicide) and helps us in exploring cosmic views and human world after we left this world. After we reach Enlightenment and left this world, there exist only Us, the energy of our Heart and Enlightening Consciousness. After His enlightenment, Arhat Thich Thong Lac was able to give us a much clearer explanation of Enlightening Consciousness. Nowadays, however, many Buddhist practitioners still misunderstand that Enlightening Consciousness is Awareness. Awareness here means the capacity of distinguishing between right and wrong, good and bad.

(2) Subconscious Mind is a flattering servant, thus it has corrupted and descending tendencies. Subconscious Mind always find ways to satisfy our urges and desires so that our body and mind can stay in states of gratification as long as they can. As a result, we are drawn into an endless cascade of temptations and desires, and forever live in a mass whirlpool of suffering which we have mistaken to be the ultimate contentment. Actually, when we sink in vice, our Wisdom

is paralyzed and unable to develop anymore and we become no more than an animal. It might already be too late if we ever got woken up and realized that we are too addicted to those delusions and have no energy left to overcome sufferings. Our life is no better than a sick person writhing in agony begging for DEATH THE SOONER THE BETTER.

Can Conscious Mind be killed? Yes. Like a patient in a coma, vegetative state, he/she does not know anything, or a patient suffering from mental disorder.

CAN THE SUBCONSCIOUS MIND BE KILLED? No. We would die if our Subconscious Mind is killed. A better way to understand is the metaphor of a king. A king can kill loyal courtiers without threatening his life or his throne; however, killing a flattering courtier would cost him his throne or even his life.

HENCE, what would we do once we

realized that our subconsciousness is a bunch of flatterers who are there to harm us? Well, we have to cultivate wisdom practices in order to educate our heart about the destructive influences of our subconsciousness so that our heart would abandon its tendencies to follow it anymore. Once our heart is detached from the sway of the subconscious mind, the subconscious mind can no longer harm our life. Master Thanh Thien has discovered something special: When our heart has become dispassionate with the subconsciousness, the subconscious mind could no longer incite us and is impossible to operate. Naturally, it turns around and follows dharma practice and thus, it helps us in executing the Dharma throughout the 6 days before our death. Certain practitioners can reach enlightenment right at this very moment. Throughout the Buddha's era, many Buddhists have reached enlightenment at their near-death moments, including the Buddha's father.

2- Why did arhat Thich Thong Lac fail to disseminate true Dharma to American monks?

(1) First off, it is necessary to affirm that the American monks do not practice Buddhism for fame and profit. There remain some monks in Vietnam who embrace a vain dream that "I PRACTICE BUDDHISM FOR THE BENEFIT OF OTHER SUFFERING PEOPLE!" American people practice absolutely for their own benefits. They are already successful in terms of career and wealth, then they decide to leave the ephemeral prosperity to follow and practice the True Principle.

(2) Then why did not the American monks accept the Buddha Dharma?

This is an issue that Bhiksu Thanh Thien need to clearly explain in order to make everyone understand how the Subconscious Mind harms our life!

To Tell The Truth! At that time, Bhiksu Thanh Thien had yet to practice Buddhism and still had doubts in Venerable Thich Thong Lac. When hearing that American monks came to Vietnam to seek guidance from the Venerable, Bhiksu Thanh Thien was very glad, because Bhiksu Thanh Thien hoped that the Americans were open minded and could uncover the truth. But the American monks did not uncover anything. They were distrustful and did not believe one bit in the Venerable's Teachings. At the same time, they were frustrated thinking that the Venerable were a malign monk!

The main reason is that American monks follow The Mahayana's desirous practices. They have embedded the image of Amitabha Buddha deeply into their subconscious mind. To them Amitabha Buddha were Real. They are addicted to Amitabha Buddha, thus their Wisdom is paralyzed and they could no longer differentiate right and wrong, truth and untruth. If the Venerable glorified Amitabha Buddha, they would have listened and praised him as a saint. But as the Venerable stated that Amitabha Buddha is fake and created by the Chinese, they immediately turned away and considered the Venerable as a malign monk and their enemy! They are like people addicted to heroin or deeply mystified by love. There is no Remedy for their addiction!

3- A story about president Bill Clinton

(1) During Clinton presidency, US and international scientists completed a documentary to disclose to mankind that Jesus was unreal, and instead, he was a Buddhist monk who had not reached enlightenment dwelling in the towering Himalayan mountains of India.

(2) The Pope and cardinal council accepted their error and decided to disperse

global Catholicism altogether, and tried to convert it into RESCUE CENTERS. And the Pope resigned. However, their attempts failed, due to overcrowded superstitious Catholic laypeople and due to the dioceses' power and financial impacts over the governments and officials in many countries. With such huge benefits, no one followed the Pope's wish and they elected a new one.

(3) Clinton knew about the unbelievable story of unreal God; he then renounced Christianity and came to Buddhism. However, it's such a misfortune for Bill Clinton that even though he's avoided the fabricated God, he has then entangled himself in an unreal, senseless Buddha, Amitabha. Such a pity!

(4) It would be good if at that time someone took Mr. Clinton to Venerable Thich Thong Lac! Since Mr. Clinton did not know about the fake Amitabha Buddha, he could have followed

the True Buddha Dharma. And because Mr. Clinton is a linguist and a lawyer, he would be able to use proper American language to help Americans to clearly understand Buddhism, then Buddhism would be promoted strongly in the U.S. As a result, the Correct Doctrine of the Buddha would Never Be Swamped with heresy.

(5) Because of not having an instructor to teach him the True Dharma, Mr. Clinton invited a Chinese monk who followed Mahayana's desirous practices[1] to be his instructor. When we knew about this, it was too late. Mr. Clinton has been infatuated with an insensible stone named Amitabha Buddha. The Subconscious Mind has harmed Mr. Clinton's spiritual life!

---

1. Those monks do not target final emancipation/ liberation like the Buddha did. Instead, they hide in the monk cloak to chase wealth and fame and lead Buddhist followers to shadowy superstitious path.

(6) Why would the Americans have an easier time practicing Buddhism if they know the True Dharma?

a) They are used to being alone. When newly born, a baby stays in his/her own room and does not sleep in the same room with his/her parents. When playing, he/she plays alone in a room and does not mingle with others.

b) They have a view that they would lead their own life without being too emotionally tightened and attached like Vietnamese people. Thus, they can easily shed the fetters of family fondness unlike Vietnamese people. The parents take responsibility to raise their children until they graduate high school. Their children have to take student loans for higher education. If they decide to work then, they can take many jobs because at high school they are already trained to work. Parents often donate their assets to charities instead of giving to their children and grandchildren because their children are already successful in their career.

c) Americans have experienced (financial and material) satisfaction, they do not practice Buddhism to make a living like the poor in Asia or the Vietnamese people.

d) Because living in a nice society, American people have a kind nature.

e) They knew that Jesus was unreal!

They have so many advantages to practice the Dharma with ease if they are instructed by a master who is good at English and understands the Dharma correctly.

4- How did subconscious mind harm Ms. Nguyen Thi Ky's life?

During the painful and chaotic war time,

it was an EXCEPTIONAL YET REAL CASE that a woman - without her husband or another man beside - fed a whole family of 30 people including children and elders and carried them around to avoid bombs and artilleries.

To find a way to save the country, her husband had travelled to France to study, graduated to be a barrister, then got assassinated. Her sons-in-law and her sons left the family to follow the Resistance! She alone shouldered the whole family.

Though being a woman, she was smart and very entrepreneurial. She opened a grocery store, instructed workers dying cloth, tailored clothes and sold buns and cookies made by workers under her instructions. Incomes from those works were sufficient for her to feed the whole family.

(4) Unfortunately, while taking care of the big family during the war time, she was pressured by a monk to feed him and his gang.

On the one hand, he sent people to vandalize her business. On the other hand, he had others spread the word that she should donate to his pagoda to have the monks bewitch anyone trying to harm her. She ground teeth to donate to the pagoda in order to protect peace for her family.

(5) Since then the subconscious mind had harmed her life. She knew that the Amitabha Buddha was fake because if he were real, he would not have let the monks do such damaging things. But for her family's peace, she had to go to the pagoda and PRETENDED TO RECITE THE AMITABHA BUDDHA SUTRA.

(6) She said, awkwardly she knew the Amitabha Buddha was fake and that she PRETENDED to practice in order to be safe, so that she could take care the whole family. But unfortunately, after over 20 years PRETENDING TO RECITE THE NAME OF

AMITABHA BUDDHA, she had the image of the fake Amitabha Buddha embedded in her mind! When realizing this, she wanted to get rid of the image from her mind but she DID NOT KNOW HOW. She tried to forget it but the image kept hovering more in her mind. She often dreamed of the Amitabha Buddha taking her to fairyland!

She said that she lived miserably, like a woman who's (mistakenly) in love with a bandit. She wanted to escape but was unable to. She said if only she thought the Amitabha Buddha to be real and she lived in delusion, she would be in peace. But she could not do that because she knew clearly that the Amitabha Buddha was fake. She had to live in torment until she died!

Now thank to Arhat Thich Thong Lac everyone knows that the SUBCONSCIOUS MIND HAS HARMED OUR LIFE!

5 - Now as we know that the subconscious mind harms our life, how can we escape from delusion?

As he practiced the Buddha Drama, Bhiksu Thanh Thien has found a method to get rid of delusions from his mind. When our mind is bored of and no longer welcomes delusions, they will automatically leave our mind, we will be at peace and can live optimistically and happily.

(1) Some malicious monks practice to actively strengthen their subconscious mind. As their subconscious mind becomes much stronger than Buddhist followers', these monks will have much easier time persuading and manipulating other Buddhists, particularly women. Those followers believe whatever they say and do whatever they tell them to do. They do so in fear mixed with unconscious zeal. They also take advantage of the Buddhist

followers' passion over Amitabha Buddha in order to manipulate them.

a) Bhiksu Thanh Thien has witnessed in Vietnam a Mahayana monk threatened and coerced a woman to submit $100,000 to him within one week. It is unbelievable but true. It is not easy at all to get $100,000 within one week in Vietnam. Yet, the woman somehow managed to get the money within one week so that the malicious monk could send his brother to the U.S for education. However, due to his brother's lack of fundamentals, his brother could not complete the education. When he used up the money, he returned to Vietnam, became a monk, held and perform ceremonial rituals to get money from naive Buddhist followers as a way of living.

b) If Buddhist followers want to get rid of the image of malicious monks from their mind, they should constantly keep thinking that those are malicious people, not decent monks, or they should think of other sentences that work with their mind. They should keep repeating the sentence in mind until their mind is sick of the image of malicious monks, then the image (or the passion toward the monks) will leave their mind.

c) It is important that once you are free from those malicious monks, don't come back to them. Because they are afraid of being uncovered and confronted by Buddhist followers, some monks may even kill them to cover the truth.

(2) Some corrupted politicians are the same. With their very strong mind, they take advantage of others' patriotism and easily manipulate people. To get rid of those people, you need to do similarly by calmly think that: after finishing the fight, those indecent guys build their own gangs to

strengthen their position and live in luxury while ignoring the poor.

(3) The same applies to love. You should repeat the thought such as: THAT PERSON IS NOT FOR ME. Within three months, the image of the lover will disappear from our mind.

(4) What about fake Amitabha Buddha? There could be two sentences for you to keep in mind.

- NAMAH AMITABHA AN INSENSIBLE STONE, or

- AMITABHA BUDDHA IS FAKE. WHY SHOULD I BELIEVE (IN) HIM?

You should keep repeating the sentences until your mind is so familiar with them that it is fed up with Amitabha, then the Amitabha image will disappear.

(5) In dealing with emotions when knowing that our family member is about to

pass away, from this moment, everyone should start singing the following lyric: I SEND YOU OFF FOR FIGHTING CHA CHA CHA. Thanks to that practice, when our family member passes away we can accept the fact and hold the funeral in calmness. Most importantly, we can then continue living in peace without being so tormented by grief.

(6) So, how should Vietnamese people think of death in order for us to bid farewell to our family member in peace? Everyone should follow Bhiksu Thanh Thien's viewpoint: I am happy for him/her now that he/she can go to have a new better life. Everyone should have such mindset, then they can feel at peace when they farewell their family member. No more UNNECESSARY grieves and torments.

(7) The viewpoint that the deceased leaves this world to have better life IS NOT SUPERSTITIOUS. That is a truth because:

a) Those having conducted evil actions will have consequences and pay for their actions. During this time, if they have a chance to meet True Buddha Dharma and determined to practice it, they can then overcome sufferings.

b) Those have conducted good actions will be reborn in prosperous family or in a developed country to experience their blessings. While being there, if they meet True Buddha Dharma and ready to drop those ephemeral blessings and practice True Buddha Dharma, they can escape the rebirth. Let's wish them the best, for their and our happiness.

(8) Westerners, particularly American people, have very simple viewpoint. When hearing that one of their family members passed away, they calmly receive the news and think that HE/SHE IS SO HAPPY TO RETURN TO GOD. Then they accept the fact with peace

and continue living their life without torment or pain. Some people are sad for a few minutes. That's all. Some families even tell funny stories about the departed so that everyone can laugh to forget their sadness. Also, they do not organize useless anniversaries for the deceased. They want people to actively take care of their own happiness and thrive joyfully in life. It is more practical and helpful to take care of yourself while you are still alive than being sad and downhearted, which just HARMS YOUR OWN LIFE and burdens people next to you. That's not worthwhile.

This technique is called Critical Thinking on Wise Attention taught by the Buddha which Bhiksu Thanh Thien has effectively practiced. People should practice it and will experience magnificent results.

6– How was Bhiksu Thanh Thien able to practice the venerable's teachings so effectively while still in doubt of the venerable?

(1) To be honest, Bhiksu Thanh Thien was also poisoned by Mahayana's mystifications of truth and untruth, real and fake. Bhiksu Thanh Thien also experienced the same feeling as others. Because his beliefs were challenged, Bhiksu Thanh Thien was shocked and felt upset on hearing the Venerable Thong Lac's teachings which contradicted those of the profound Great Vehicle of Mahayana! However, Bhiksu Thanh Thien restrained his anger and was determined to find the truth.

(2) How could Bhiksu Thanh Thien find the truth with his secular eyes?

a) Throughout direct meetings with people, the Venerable Thong Lac appeared very casual and down to earth, much less

SOLEMN and MAJESTIC than Mahayana monks who know how to play their role!

b) In his speech, the Venerable Thong Lac neither took verbal precautions nor tried to persuade. He said what he thought and meant, and he did not care if listeners believed in what he said or not. As Bhiksu Thanh Thien was not attracted to the Venerable's sayings, how could he believe in him?

c) At that time, Bhiksu Thanh Thien decided to secretly observe the Venerable's lifestyle. Bhiksu Thanh Thien found that the Venerable has a simple life. He took one meal per day and worked continuously in peace and equanimity throughout the day. Then Bhiksu Thanh Thien believed in him a bit.

d) The Venerable told Bhiksu Thanh Thien that THERE WERE NO SUPERNATURAL THINGS or INVISIBLE SPIRIT WORLDS. Bhiksu Thanh Thien then stayed in a cemetery on cold, windy and rainy nights. He was cold but not feared. He clearly observed through those nights that illusions of ghosts were born from our fears while in fact there weren't ghosts. He then believed in the Venerable a bit more.

e) THE BEST PATHWAY IS TO CONFIRM WHETHER THE VENERABLE'S TEACHINGS ARE RIGHT OR WRONG IS TO PRACTICE THEM.

7- How to practice (the true Buddha Dharma)?

(1) Firstly, Bhiksu Thanh Thien sincerely pays tribute to Ms Ut Dieu Quang who awakened him by a short sentence: THEN YOU SIT FOR ONE MINUTE ONLY!

It happened when Bhiksu Thanh Thien entered Chon Nhu Monastery to learn practicing (Buddhism). Bhiksu Thanh Thien wrongly THOUGHT THAT PEOPLE COULD

PRACTICE THEN I ALSO COULD PRACTICE. Like other practitioners, he was assigned with a hermitage to practice alone and was constantly attacked by his Subconscious Mind. Particularly, it was impossible to sit in the lotus position. It was so painful to put two legs cross each other. Frustrated, Bhiksu Thanh Thien left his hermitage to go to the kitchen for a break. He met Ms Ut Dieu Quang and complained: UT, I COULD NOT SIT STILL IN LOTUS POSITION BECAUSE MY LEGS WERE SO SORE. Ms. Ut immediately responded: THEN YOU SIT FOR ONE MINUTE ONLY! Wow! SO GLAD. It was due to this awakening sentence that Bhiksu Thanh Thien FOUND THE METHOD OF GRADUAL PROGRESSION, meaning we practice gradually to make our mind familiar with sitting still for one minute. When the mind is familiar with the practice, we can increase the sitting time to 5 minutes, then to the whole day, without having sore or numb legs. People should try this method! This is indeed a PRACTICAL, SCIENTIFIC method that Bhiksu Thanh Thien has created and shared with people in order to help themselves in their self-rescue and self-defeat quest!

(2) Ever since, Bhiksu Thanh Thien has been practicing the method of critical thinking on wise attention taught by the Venerable and the gradual progression method inspired by Ms. Ut Dieu Quang's statement. It is magnificent. By effectively combining the two methods, Bhiksu Thanh Thien has step by step practiced successfully with THE JOY OF SELF-DEFEAT.

8– While not yet believing in the venerable, how was Bhiksu Thanh Thien able to proceed his practice to success?

(1) Firstly, it is a big mistake if we use

our secular eyes to judge a saint through his appearance! As holy people are not performance artists, they neither play role nor try to mince their words to seduce, attract or persuade people. That's why people are often attracted to and believe in artists while suspecting saints, the noble beings. Buddha Shakyamuni faced the same suspect. With his skeleton-like body covered by tattered clothes, Buddha Shakyamuni firmly STATED: "In the heavens above and the earth beneath I alone am the honored one, the deva of the world wisdom, Four Sufferings of birth, old-age, sickness and death. I AM THE ONLY BUDDHA IN THIS WORLD." Would anyone dare to believe that BUDDHA SHAKYAMUNI was a saint, an Enlightened being, then? Everyone at that time thought that he was an evil and malicious monk! THERE WERE VERY FEW PEOPLE who believed in him. Even after the Buddha had trained hundreds of Arhats, many people still had doubts in him and followed provocations of malicious monks to smear His name and to stain His reputation, and even attempted to kill him. They were the same type of brainless people currently vilifying Arhat Thich Thong Lac.

(2) The only way to have faith in His teachings is to practice them accordingly. The end RESULT is the best answer.

(3) However, we should not practice because of our trust in the Venerable Thong Lac. Instead, we should TRUST OURSELVES. The Buddha taught clearly that YOU SHOULD NOT BELIEVE IN ME. "I am only the guide. You must be the one who decides to follow the guide or not. You should believe in yourself". Arhat Thich Thong Lac taught: SAVE YOURSELF. No one else can save you!

9- Firstly, Bhiksu Thanh Thien practiced quitting alcoholism

If we do not quit alcoholism, how can we practice (Buddhism) while we're drunk? Bhiksu Thanh Thien was seriously addicted to alcohol for 40 years, consuming between 32 – 38 cans of beer each day. Figuratively, his blood was full of beer. How could Thanh Thien, being so addicted to alcohol, depravities and fornication, practice (Buddhism) successfully? Only would mad people believe that!

Bhiksu Thanh Thien practiced alcohol rehabilitation by:

a) Day and night, he constantly and ceaselessly reminded himself that: "I had to quit alcohol; drinking was not of any help but making me mad, swear, utter dirty words and conduct fornication. Bhiksu Thanh Thien blamed himself, accused himself and were determined to abandon drinking. He continued drinking while executing the critical thinking on this wise attention.

b) He continuously blamed and accused himself and were determined to quit alcoholism. After three months of constant reminding, A MIRACLE HAPPENED TO HIM. Bhiksu Thanh Thien felt sick of drinking and did not want to drink anymore. Then he stated that he would STOP DRINKING FROM THEN ON, and he did.

c) Wow! It sounds unbelievable but that's true. From that day on, Bhiksu Thanh Thien's passion for alcohol was completely exhausted. He sat among drinkers, but he did not take any beer! He still ate meat, though.

d) It was such a huge happiness! I can defeat myself! I can successfully rehab. From now on, I will never be TORTURED BY the addiction! I can live happily with a peaceful and tranquil mind! I am sincerely grateful to Venerable Thong Lac who taught me to RESCUE MYSELF.

Dear Venerable, I have saved myself! Then Bhiksu Thanh Thien believed in Venerable Thong Lac a bit more.

e) Also at that time, Bhiksu Thanh Thien found out that: If we constantly think critically about drinking - its harmful effects on our body, mind and life - until our mind is imbued with the attention to quit alcoholism and sick of drinking, we can then QUIT DRINKING. It is so easy and truly peaceful. IT IS MAGNIFICENT! I HAVE SUCCESSFULLY QUITTED ALCOHOLISM! I HAVE defeated my depraved self! Everyone should try this method! This is a scientific and practical method that everyone needs to be implemented to their quest of self-defeat and self-rescue. This is the method of CRITICAL THINKING ON WISE ATTENTION taught by the Buddha, which is MISUNDERSTOOD and wrongly perceived as SELF-INSINUATION by Mahayana monks.

The method of critical thinking on wise attention as taught by the Buddha is truly amazing. By practicing this method, we train our mind so that it gets sick of things that we want to get rid of or so that it can acknowledge and welcome ideas/wisdom that we like to cultivate. Once the critical thinking of certain intention is completed and embedded in our mind, we can easily turn it into actions. IT SOUNDS UNBELIEVABLE BUT IT'S TRUE!

For millions of times, I would like to pay tribute to Venerable Thong Lac who had taught me, A DRUNK, to DEFEAT and RESCUE MYSELF, and progress toward LIBERATING myself from suffering! Namo Venerable Thich Thong Lac.

10 – Develop self-cultivating method

(1) Wow! Thank to the Venerable Thong Lac's teachings, PLAYBOY Thanh Thien has successfully SAVED and DEFEATED HIMSELF. How delightful! As he has abandoned alcoholism, Bhiksu Thanh Thien felt as if he were flying above the clouds and enjoying the sweet joy of SELF-RESCUE AND SELF-DEFEAT! From that success, Bhiksu Thanh Thien WENT FURTHER in developing A SELF-CULTIVATING PROTOCOL!

(2) Why did Bhiksu Thanh Thien develop his practicing method while Venerable Thong Lac has already taught the Buddhists how to practice?

a) Because right after Bhiksu Thanh Thien started practicing Buddhism more seriously, the Venerable suddenly passed away!

b) IT IS ABSOLUTELY IMPOSSIBLE for a person to follow Venerable Thong Lac's teachings without knowing how to practice. It is absolutely impossible for a newbie to practice the Venerable's teaching.

c) Because Venerable Thong Lac did not explain how to practice and where to start. He assumed people who sought His teachings have already had some experience with Buddhist practices.

Some examples include:

1. The Venerable told the practitioners to practice solitude in their own hermitage. How exactly is living in solitude? That is not easy at all if the practitioner did not (know how to) equip for himself psychologically and have some experience in Buddhist practice (of solitude). They could be severely attacked by their own haphazard, frivolous thoughts, while SELF-TALKING isn't even allowed in this kind of solitude.

2. He told practitioners to take only one

meal each day. How can they take only one meal each day while they haven't practiced so beforehand? The hunger is unbearable! Most practitioners had to hide some food from lunch for a furtive dinner to curb their hunger!

3. He told practitioners to practice relinquishment (of the attempts of the mind) in their hermitage. How to relinquish (the attempts) the mind? What does it mean by practicing relinquishment? All practitioners were DEAD WRONG. All of them follow Mahayana instructions in this practice. Yet, none of them dared to ask the Venerable to give instruction on how to conduct the practice. According to the Mahayana instructions, practicing relinquishment (of the attempts of the mind) - letting go of the mind - is to sit still and control the mind from chasing thoughts of greed, hatred, delusion, haughtiness, and doubt. That is a wrong approach because we

are INADVERTENTLY using our consciousness to restrain our mind.

4. He told practitioners to let go. HOW TO LET GO? What to let go first, or second, third? IS IT EASY to let go our familial fondness and to not miss our parents, wife, and children? Without letting go of our familial fondness, we only place one leg on the boat of True Buddha Dharma while our other leg is still on the boat of secular life. (Practicing Buddhism while we refuse to let go of our affinities is impossible. One can't have the cake and eat it too!). In the end, neither our secular life nor secluded life will be successful!

ANNEX

(1) How to practice solitude?

- What does "SOLITUDE" mean (in Buddhism)?

According to the Buddha's teachings, solitude means that our six senses focus only on our body.

- How to practice solitude in accordance with the Buddha's teachings?

We must practice MINDFULNESS.

- How to practice MINDFULNESS?

It means that our mind focuses on our body, from toe to head and from head to toe, throughout our entire body, and that we know clearly what we are doing. When we eat, we know that we are eating, what we are eating and whether we are chewing quickly or slowly. We must always know every movement of our body in every second, non-stop. To be able to do this, we must (first) practice this method within very short time daily in order to train our mind to get used to the practice, then we gradually extend the practice time. As we conduct the practice suitably to our capacity to absorb it and the practice time is gradually extended, we would find our path toward achieving enlightenment. Each person has his or her own time for finding the path. No one is the same as others. If you wish to succeed in practicing MINDFULNESS, you should practice the six basic methods taught by Bhiksu Thanh Thien beforehand. Once you have mastered the six basic methods, you can easily practice MINDFULNESS.

- How should we practice solitude?

Each day, we must practice sitting still alone in a room for 10 minutes without talking with anyone, listening, reading, or watching (anything). After a while, as our mind becomes familiar with the practice, we gradually extend the practice time. Eventually, once we can extend our solitude up to six months without chasing thoughts and we have mastered the six basic methods, then it is only a matter of TIME before we reach enlightenment.

(2) How to take only one meal per day?

For instance, you are taking 04 meals per day. You should firstly bring our attention to reducing to 03 meals per day. Once you mind has become familiar with this thought, you can then start taking 03 meals per day. Gradually, you can reduce to only 1 meal per day. Remember to practice critical thinking on the attention until your mind is familiar with the new idea before you start cutting down the number of meals. Don't rush or you will fail. As you have successfully taken only 1 meal per day, you should keep reminding yourself on the attention that you want to maintain the lifestyle of one meal per day in order to prevent your mind from forgetting.

(3) What does "relinquishment (of the attempts of the mind)" mean?

Relinquishing (the attempts of) the mind means to abandon (the sway of) desires and evil temptations and cultivating wholesomeness. Anger, resentment, afflictions, and desires, ... are EVIL. Now we practice abandoning those evil deeds and following the Path of Righteousness. As we completely follow the Path of Righteousness and absolutely get rid of evil deeds, our mind becomes peaceful, tranquil, and worry-free. By that time, our mind is no longer disturbed. Therefore, evil tendencies can no longer affect our mind, just like water off a duck's back.

- How to practice leaving desires and evil temptations in order to relinquish the (urges of the) mind?

We should practice critical thinking on wise attention to make our mind familiar with the thought of leaving the temptations and following the Path of Virtue. Temptations will gradually be driven away by the critical thinking. ISN'T THAT FABULOUS?

(4) Let go. How to let go?

Practitioners only need to diligently practice critical thinking on wise attention and the six basic methods until they master them. AS THE RESULT, practitioners will effectively let go of their affinities toward family, wealth, fame, house and land. This comes from Bhiksu Thanh Thien's experience. Critical Thinking on Wise Attention should be skillfully integrated into the practice of the six basic methods as instructed by Bhiksu Thanh Thien. Once our mind has been familiar with the six basic methods, our guilt of mistakes in the past would have already left our mind. With that said, we already have been able to separate (our mind) from urges, desires, and evil tendencies while cultivated wholesomeness, and walked our Path of Righteousness, with the adamant will of refusal to cause suffering to ourselves, other people and all living beings as our moral compass. We can then easily let go (of our affinities) and achieve enlightenment. That pathway is as clear as in Venerable Thong Lac's teachings.

CRITICAL THINKING ON WISE ATTENTION AND THE SIX BASIC METHODS:

1) Sitting in lotus position
2) Practicing solitude retreat
3) Breathing meditation
4) Walking meditation
5) Sagacity meditation - (practiced at leisure times)
6) Taking one meal per day

(3) Bhiksu Thanh Thien continued practicing critical thinking on wise attention and started practicing the six basic methods. He practiced each method separately so that they become more intuitive before practicing them in combination.

(4) At the beginning, Bhiksu Thanh Thien only took the practices leisurely as a kind of exercise because he thought that he was THE MOST IMMORAL, DIRTY AND DEPRAVED PERSON IN THE WORLD who should never dream of achieving enlightenment. Though he took the practices leisurely, he conducted them regularly. It was UNBELIEVABLE BUT TRUE that the practices gradually embedded in his mind.

(5) Determined to practice vegetarianism. Being a devil who had been habitually and addictively eating animal flesh for over 70 years, HOW COULD BHIKSU THANH THIEN PRACTICE VEGETARIANISM?

a) Bhiksu Thanh Thien continued eating animal flesh while continuously and constantly remind himself that: "I WANT TO to be a vegetarian; eating animal flesh is so disgusting and cruel! They also have the right to live and need to live as much as I do." He kept reminding himself with this attention until one day, Bhiksu Thanh Thien entered a restaurant. Surprisingly, that was a vegetarian restaurant. Oh! That was a full-moon day. He thought it was good to take a vegetarian meal then. Bhiksu Thanh Thien had not taken vegetarian meals during new moon or full-moon day (or any day) since his mother passed away. So, he did not notice that day was a full-moon day. He just ordered a vegetarian meal.

b) WOW! It was amazing! He did not know why but Bhiksu Thanh Thien felt that the vegetarian meal tasted SO DELICIOUS. When he returned home, he no longer felt

ANXIOUS or UNCOMFORTABLE. Instead, he felt extremely relaxed.

c) It sounds strange but it was true. Before leaving home for a usual (aimless) wander, as Bhiksu Thanh Thien has retired, he often had breakfast. On that day, waiting for him at home was a steaming and eye-catching bowl of Hue beef noodles. But strangely, Bhiksu Thanh Thien did not feel attracted to it. Instead, he left home and bought a portion of steamed sticky rice with peanuts for his breakfast. From that day on, Bhiksu Thanh Thien no longer ate animal flesh. He followed the exemplary masters on vegetarianism. How wonderful is that, the devil who used to eat animal flesh has successfully changed to eating vegetables. Bhiksu Thanh Thien was so happy because HE HAS RESCUED HIMSELF AND DEFEATED HIMSELF!

d) IT IS so INCREDIBLE! So delightful!

Bhiksu Thanh Thien started to realize how magical Critical Thinking on Wise Attention was! Bhiksu Thanh Thien only needed to constantly think I WANT TO PRACTICE VEGETARIANISM until his mind was fond of the idea, then he took vegetarian meals and felt that they tasted delicious and he no longer felt anxious as he used to.

e) This is a PRACTICAL AND SCIENTIFIC method. Anyone can practice it. Everyone should try these methods so that you can taste the sweetness of SELF-RESCUE and SELF-DEFEAT. IT SOUNDS UNBELIEVABLE, BUT IT'S TRUE.

11- About practicing critical thinking on wise attention and the six basic methods

(1) After having succeeded in practicing vegetarianism, Bhiksu Thanh Thien was very happy because this was another difficult challenge that he has managed to master, and especially he could DEFEAT and RESCUE HIMSELF from the evil karma of eating animal flesh!

(2) As he became comfortable with vegetarianism, Bhiksu Thanh Thien began to shift attention toward changing his habit of taking 03 meals per day. Like the previous successes, Bhiksu Thanh Thien easily changed the habit once his mind became comfortable and imbued with the idea of reducing the number of meals. However, Bhiksu Thanh Thien DID NOT MORTIFY HIS BODY, neither did he force his heart. Whenever he felt a need of eating, he would have a little snack, such as

some crackers or fruits, to ease the need. Then he brought his attention to the thought that it was not necessary to have those snacks. After a few times, he quit the snacks altogether. He then cut down from 03 meals per day to 02 meals, then to 01 meal, SMOOTHLY and PEACEFULLY.

(3) Once he was comfortable with only 01 meal per day, Bhiksu Thanh Thien DOUBLE-CHECKED to see if the diet had any adverse effects to his body. He went to a FITNESS CENTER and exercised as hard as professional athletes in addition to 06-hour walking meditation. In total, he had 08 hours of physical activities. He felt that his body was healthy and strong. That means he could take 01 meal per day and that diet mechanism did not cause any harmful effect to his body.

12 – Long distance walking meditation

(1) As Bhiksu Thanh Thien had many serious diseases, including diabetes and swollen feet, it was so difficult and discouraging for him to practice walking meditation in short distance as taught by Venerable Thong Lac, which is to take 10 steps, then sit down, and start walking 10 steps again. He felt lazy and sleepy.

(2) Bhiksu Thanh Thien invented the practice of walking meditation in long distance. It is amazing, long distance walking meditation has many incredible advantages.

a) At the beginning, the daily practice session for 06 basic methods was too short - only a few minutes, Bhiksu Thanh Thien had lots of vacant time which he felt unsettled and didn't know what to do with it. Thanks to long distance walking meditation, his vacant time was well spent!

b) Long distance walking meditation helps Bhiksu Thanh Thien turn the practice of critical thinking on wise attention into a habit. While walking, Bhiksu Thanh Thien experimented several different statements that helped his mind become comfortable with certain wise attentions. For instance: "I KNOW THAT I AM EXERCISING WALKING MEDITATION, walk firmly (in order) to strengthen my legs and soften the ground, walk (in order) to stabilize my mind and achieve enlightenment,... 1, 2, 3, 4, 5 (count along the steps)". Then he changed to another sentence: "MY MIND IS ADAMANT AGAINST ALL EVIL TEMPTATIONS, FEELINGS AND SENSATIONS...; LEAVING GREED, ANGER AND IGNORANCE WILL END SUFFERINGS; contemplation on abandoning greed, contemplation on abandoning anger, contemplation on abandoning ignorance." Then he focused to another sentence: "SEXUAL DESIRE MUST LEAVE MY BODY,

DIABETES MUST LEAVE MY BODY, I NEED TO TAKE ONE MEAL PER DAY TO ADVANCE FURTHER IN MY QUEST OF PURIFICATION" Bhiksu Thanh Thien kept on repeating those sentences again and again throughout his walking meditation session.

c) Practicing critical thinking on wise attention helps us STOP RANDOM THOUGHTS.

d) Long-distance walking meditation prevents sleepiness.

e) Long-distance walking meditation prevents laziness.

g) Long-distance walking meditation helps us STRENGTHEN OUR WILLPOWER FOR our liberating quest.

h) With this willpower, he gained joyfulness in practicing walking meditation for short distance as taught by Venerable Thong Lac and executed it more easily.

It was unexpected that the practice EFFECTIVELY MITIGATED and PREVENTED SEVERAL DISEASES. Bhiksu Thanh Thien started practicing walking meditation for 15 minutes. When his mind became more familiar with the practice, he gradually increased the time up to six hours per day. Long-distance walking meditation sessions help prevent diseases better than short walking meditation sessions.

i) With 6 hours of long-distance walking meditation daily, Bhiksu Thanh Thien had also tried walking non-stop for 24 hours, twice. He felt completely happy and peaceful. His health is good. His MIND is clear, healthy and free from confusion.

k) While walking meditation, Bhiksu Thanh Thien does not HYPOCRITICALLY pray for not stepping on any living beings. He walks on trail and avoids stepping on living beings as much as he can, as long as that avoidance does not interrupt his practice. We would have better focus on walking and our two moving feet. We should not worry about stepping on something and looking around. That also helps prevent RANDOM THOUGHTS from emerging and causing our mind to wander.

13 – How effective is long distance walking meditation in disease treatment and prevention?

(1) Disease self-treatment methods for practitioners as taught by Venerable Thong Lac

a) Sitting upright in lotus position.

b) Breathing steadily. This is an internal movement as a focal point in meditation.

c) Moving hands up and down, or in and out, or standing up and sitting down. These are external movements to focus on in meditation. All body movements are external ones.

d)Using commands on wise attention in order to expel diseases (out of our body) by calling the disease's name and tell that it must leave this body and that "I abandon greed, anger and delusion."

As the practitioner combines these 04 practices persistently with perfect harmony, his mind will be bored of the diseases and the diseases will subsequently disappear.

Many practitioners have succeeded in expelling their diseases while practicing under Venerable Thong Lac's supervision.

(2) Disease treatment methods invented and practiced with excellent success by Bhiksu Thanh Thien

a) Bhiksu Thanh Thien invented the methods because he had so many diseases, including diabetes and swollen feet, and he did not know how to conduct (Buddhist) practices. He found that sitting still for a

LONG PERIOD was TOO CHALLENGING. Those having some experience with Buddhist practices can easily sit still because it has become habitual to them. That's why Bhiksu Thanh Thien invented the method of long-distance walking meditation.

b) The method still aligns with the principles set out by Venerable Thong Lac, including rhythmic combination of critical thinking (and commanding) on wise attention with internal and external movements in meditation, without weariness even practicing in an extensive amount of time.

c) As a result, his diabetes was cured completely. Before meeting Venerable Thong Lac, Bhiksu Thanh Thien had to stay in hospital and people worried that his leg might have to be amputated and that his eyes could become blind. Doctors prescribed long-term medication for Bhiksu Thanh Thien and said that there's no cure to this disease. When Venerable Thong Lac taught him the self-treatment methods, Bhiksu Thanh Thien practiced them and did not use the medication. After 02 years, Bhiksu Thanh Thien returned to the hospital for a comprehensive health check, including blood tests and urine test, and was concluded that NO DISEASE WAS FOUND. "How delightful, I have defeated and rescued myself!" Bhiksu Thanh Thien feels that his body becomes very healthy and NO LONGER SUFFERS FROM ACHES, TIREDNESS, LETHARGY, AND FATIGUE.

d) As Bhiksu Thanh Thien kept practicing long distance walking meditation, his foot-swelling problem disappeared without his notice! Once he recognized that the disease had ended, he felt as if HE WAS FLYING. "I have rescued and defeated myself! Couldn't be any happier!"

e) IT WAS DIFFICULT TO BELIEVE BUT TRUE that Bhiksu Thanh Thien was successful in stopping his hunger for sex! Since he was successful in changing to taking only one meal per day, Bhiksu Thanh Thien continuously repeated the thought: SEXUAL DESIRE MUST LEAVE ME, I don't need you anymore, leaving greed, anger and delusion. After one year, Bhiksu Thanh Thien found out that he no longer desired sex. HOW TO KNOW IF THAT WAS TRUE? Bhiksu Thanh Thien visited a joy house where he used to stop by. Once seeing Bhiksu Thanh Thien enter the place, women immediately surrounded him, invited him to sit, caressed him, flirted softly and sweetly while opening a bottle of scrumptious wine. Meanwhile, Bhiksu Thanh Thien felt indifferent and his mind was imperturbable. He no longer felt the desire for WOMEN. To be surer, Bhiksu Thanh Thien sat there for 15 minutes to observe if his mind was truly imperturb or he had to consciously control his mind. It was true that his mind was no longer moved. He was so delighted. He paid the bill and tips, then happily left the place. "How delightful. I have liberated myself from suffering!"

g) "Oh Master, I practice (Buddhism) in order to be free from SUFFERINGS. I pay tribute to you (the teacher) thousands and millions of times for your teachings on the True Buddhism which have saved me. Dear Master, I have rescued myself, defeated myself and liberated my life from ALL SUFFERINGS!"

Overrun by joy, it felt as if his body was gently wrapped by and bathed in the scents of a rainbow of colorful flowers falling from the skies; and with a gust of wind the fragrance permeated throughout the atmosphere as if it wanted everyone to share Bhiksu Thanh Thien's happiness of self-rescue. self-defeat and self-liberalization. WOW! It was so fabulous!

"Master, in order to show my honor and tribute to you, I voluntarily spread your teachings and share my practicing experience, my gnosis, to people who SEEK TRUE BUDDHIST TEACHING so that people can understand and practice the True Buddha Dharma as you have wished. Everyone, let's practice together in order to rescue ourselves, defeat ourselves and liberate our life from ALL SUFFERINGS right in this very life, and wait no longer for the next life. At the same time, we should maintain, spread and promote the True Buddha Dharma to others and next generations, so that True Buddhism won't be overshadowed by heresies (or the so-called Buddhist teaching) and so that Venerable Thong Lac's efforts and devotion to humankind won't be wasted and betrayed.

DEAR SENIOR LADIES AND GENTLEMEN

(I believe that) You have been through lots of twists and turns in your life. With your bountiful experience, you know what is right and what is wrong. It is the most precious time now that Arhat Thich Thong Lac appeared and enlightened us on True Buddha Dharma. He taught us SELF-RESCUE and SELF-DEFEAT in order to help us liberate our life from all sufferings. You are even luckier that you have Bhiksu Thanh Thien who voluntarily explains Arhat Thich Thong Lac's teachings in comprehensible colloquial, prosaic language and also shares his successful practice experiences in order to bolster your journey toward enlightenment. Now that you have relieved yourselves from the burdens of family, career and societal responsibilities, each of you may have UNDERSTOOD thoroughly THE RIDICULOUSNESS OF THE EPHEMERALITY OF LIFE! EVERYTHING IN LIFE IS NOTHING BUT AN ILLUSION! Each of you are quietly counting your days as you inevitably approach closer to your imminent death. So instead of wasting your free time with frivolous matters, why don't you put your time into good use by practicing True Buddha Dharma so that you can defeat your (decadent, evil) self, rescue and liberate your life from all sufferings?

It is important that you joyfully experiment your life and share your experience to your children and grandchildren; they would appreciate that for life! Your results will be the evidence and the answer for your offspring to whether the Buddha Dharma resurrected by Venerable Thich Thong Lac and instructed by Bhiksu Thanh Thien is TRUE or FALSE! If it is false, the youngsters will certainly throw it (the practice) into trash bin. If it is proven true, this would be a precious opportunity once in a thousand years, our posterity will practice, protect, maintain, and promote it, and so, TRUE Buddha Dharma will be further spread to enlighten suffering souls everywhere.

It is precious and HARD TO BELIEVE BUT TRUE that if you practice True Buddha Dharma correctly, your aging progress may still be unavoidable but for sure each of you will live in peace and equanimity with abundant health and CLEAR MIND until your last breath. You will leave this world with the joy of "I HAVE LIBERATED MY LIFE FROM ALL SUFFERINGS".

The only enlightened master in this world is sincerely instructing you to step by step progress toward self-rescue, self-defeat and self-liberation AS PER THE BUDDHA'S TEACHINGS.

GOOD NEWS!

True Buddha Dharma is reaching out to you!

At the beginning when Bhiksu Thanh Thien started to disseminate TRUE BUDDHA DHARMA resurrected by Arhat Thich Thong Lac to all people in the world through Facebook, he had also faced strong oppositions from many sides.

Up to this point, however, over 40,000 people have read his teachings on Facebook each day while only a few people disagree!

At the same time, people made over 1,223,000 visits to tuhanhdungchanhphatphap.net on Facebook and Youtube in order to get to know the True Buddha Dharma.

Bhiksu Thanh Thien sincerely thanks goodwill people and technical specialists in providing him with supports for Facebook, Youtube.

Bhiksu Thanh Thien also sincerely thanks kindhearted people who inform this good news to other people each day, so that more and more people find the way toward the True Buddha Dharma. Everyone should encourage others to progress their practice, so that TRUE Buddha Dharma can be further spread in order to enlighten (more) suffering souls in the world and they can liberate/extricate themselves from sufferings.

ANNEX

1) People are often deceived by the idea (or misperception) that practicing Buddhism required deep understanding of the Buddha Dharma and is very difficult. They are clearly deceived by the melodious and harmonious recitations of fervent prayers. Even a 10-year-old child can conduct this practice, can't he/she?

2) People are also cheated by the idea that practicing Buddhism needed MORAL and COMPASSION. What kind of moral and compassion is mentioned here? All ambitious, desirous Mahayana monks and nuns are wrapped in GOLDEN CLOAKs like performers with sparkling outfits on stage. Their mind is

full of tricks and schemes in order to cheat naive Buddhist followers.

3) As a result, most Buddhist followers want to choose the most difficult and the most superior methods to practice. They fall into all sorts of delusions and in the end they can only resort to chanting some mantras or prayers and recite Mayahana scriptures which do not give any progress, but else can they do?

4) In fact, there is no superior or inferior methods in True Buddha Dharma. There are only practice methods that are suitable to different practitioners. Once the practitioner has perfected and imbued with the qualities cultivated by the practices he chose, the practitioner has achieved Buddhahood and liberated himself. Bhiksu Thanh Thien has been pointing out the evidence from the Nikaya scriptures that Buddha gave one

and only one method to each bhiksu. They practiced the given method until it became an indispensable part of their mind, then they achieved Enlightenment.

5) There is no need for any kind of sublime and HYPOCRITICAL moral (in order to practice Buddhism). As long as we acknowledge the Four Noble Truths and want to practice the True Buddha Dharma, we can always start practicing. Despite previous and current sins that we have involved in, including trickery, murder and robbery, if we are determined to forsake them, we can always start practicing True Buddha Dharma. Bhiksu Thanh Thien pointed to several examples such as a prostitute named Lien Hoa Sac, a hunter, a murderer, a janitor... When they met the Buddha, they learnt and acknowledged the Four Noble Truths and determined to let go of their previous sinful conducts, all of them successfully achieved Enlightenment.

6) A common critical mistake among practitioners is that they want to dress up and show off to let everybody know that they are practicing Buddha Dharma. This is merely a PRESENTATION in order to entertain other people. They are just like the ambitious and covetous Mahayana monks who flaunt their fancy golden cloak in order to deceive naive people about their practice (of Buddha Dharma) so that they can collect money (from those people). THE CLOAK DOES NOT MAKE THE MONK.

Practicing True Buddha Dharma means that we quietly cleanse our mind. When our mind is clear, tranquil and enlightened, our wisdom becomes extremely bright and sharp.

7) There are two kinds of clear mind:

(1) One kind is the mind chasing pleasures (or passion), called ignorance. For instance, doctors, engineers, lawyers and

gem specialists... These people achieve their expertise and keen mind through learning and practicing. Their gut-feeling or intuition would take charge in their work; intellect only comes in second to back it up. With their trained mind, they can cure diseases and solve issues in their expert field effectively like legends.

(2) The other kind is the mind that forsakes pleasures (or passion). As we practice the True Buddha Dharma, our mind becomes enlightened and approach closer to KNOWLEDGE OF THE TRUTH which leads us to the shore of SELF-LIBERATION.

IMPORTANT TEACHINGS

Below are important teachings of the True Buddha Dharma that you need to understand before you can begin your journey.

1) The four noble truths.

2) The eightfold noble paths.

3) 12 Linked-chain dependent originations.

4) 37 Aids conducing to enlightenment.

5) 5 Aggregates or processes within the body (skandhas).

6) Practice one method, one-method practice.

7) Long distance walking meditation.

8) Critical thinking and commanding on wise attention.

9) 6 Basic methods.

All of Bhiksu Thank Thien's sermons regarding practice instructions are available at http://tuhanhdungchanhphatphap.net/

1) The four noble truths

Introduction: Bhiksu Thanh Thien explains the True Buddha Dharma to readers with clear, affirmative and concise language in order to help readers to quickly understand the Dharma. At the same time, with his successful experience in practicing the Buddha's teachings, Bhiksu Thanh Thien tries to help practitioners to experiment those teachings for themselves, so that practitioners will never be deceived. Since he already practices those teachings successfully, Bhiksu Thanh Thien will clearly address all challenges and private problems and questions in order to help everybody to understand and overcome (them). An evidence of success is that after a series of his sermons on BREATHING MEDITATION, Bhiksu Thanh Thien has received many sincere thank-you emails and messages! That means the readers truly understand his teachings, which brings joy to Bhiksu Thanh Thien.

THE FOUR NOBLE TRUTHS

After achieving Enlightenment and discovering the Four Noble Truths, the Buddha developed practicing methods and helped EACH PERSON to conduct the methods until they have perfected and completely imbued with the qualities they have been honing and cultivating, then (the practitioner) achieved Enlightenment as the Buddha did. The Buddha preached the first sermon to Ajnata Kaudinya (Kieu Tran Nhu) and his brothers.

He instructed the five brothers and many of their fellows to conduct practicing methods until they achieved Arhatship. The sermon is about the TRUTHS that he found: THE FOUR NOBLE TRUTHS.

Buddha taught:

(1) Life is temporary and ephemeral, like flowers blooming in the morning and withering in the evening, constant sufferings due to birth, old age, sickness and death. This is **the Truth of Suffering.**

(2) The cause that leads to our sufferings of birth, old age, sickness and death, is (our) DESIRES. As we were born from our parents' DESIRES (Ignorance) and nurtured by parents and relatives' desires, we continue to be submerged in the cascading rapids of desires even when we grow up and get to know the Four Noble Truths. Since we always live in desires which include greed, anger, delusion,

arrogance and doubt, they grow very strongly and deeply within our subconscious mind. This is **the Truth of the Cause of Sufferings (Accumulation).**

(3) Do you want to extricate yourself from the sufferings? If yes, you have to practice the True Buddha Dharma to reduce your desires to minimum level. In order to reach that level, we have to master our stomach or our hunger for food. Our stomach is the root cause of our slavery to desires/hunger for pleasures! We must choose one method out of the True Buddha Dharma and keep practicing it until we are imbued with the qualities cultivated by the method, then we achieve Enlightenment and liberate ourselves from sufferings! If we stand still, we will sink. If we move forward, we will be drifted away. The only choice/ option (for us) is to cross over, meaning practicing the True Buddha Dharma until we achieve Enlightenment. Once our mind

is imbued with the qualities cultivated and honed by True Buddha Dharma, we achieve Buddhahood. This is **the Truth of The End of Suffering (Dissolution).**

(4) When you are determined to practice the True Buddha Dharma, you should firstly practice critical thinking on wise attention and deploy this practice in conducting the six basic practicing methods until you master them. Once we have mastered those methods, we should pick one specific method that's compatible to us and practice it to perfection, i.e. until the qualities become us, and thus we achieve Enlightenment. What are the choices of practicing methods? They are The Eightfold Noble Paths, The Twelve Link-Chained Arising Conditions, 37 Aids to Enlightenment, books by Venerable Thong Lac which explains the True Buddha Dharma, and the Nikaya scriptures. The Buddha said: "If you are attached to my physique/form (or rely on my

prowess) to beg me to grant you something, you will never meet Tagathata (Buddhahood or the Supreme Enlightenment). Only those who practice my teachings to perfection, they shall meet Tagathata." So the correct way is to practice the True Buddha Dharma until we achieve Buddhahood. We will then complete the work of our life! That is **the Truth of The (Right) Path**.

2) The eightfold noble paths

Do not misunderstand this teaching as per explained by Mahayana monks! They call them "eight ways". In their true meaning as taught by the Buddha, these are eight practicing methods

(1) **Proper Understanding:** We must carefully observe and scrutinize issues that concern us in order for us to confirm that we (directly) know them and that they are true

(or not). For example, when we hear that Venerable Thong Lac achieved Arhatship, we must live close to him, observe his life with our own eyes in order to verify if he is a true HOLY MONK. Asking other people about the Venerable or paying Him some visits just isn't the way to draw conclusions about His Arhatship! What would happen if we met the wrong people? We have to be the investigator for ourselves.

(2) **Proper Thinking:** Once we know the facts about certain issues, we can start evaluating and analyzing the causations as weli as the effects of the issue(s) to see if they are good or evil. If they are good, we acknowledge them. If they are evil, we ignore them. For instance, with Proper Understanding about Venerable Thong Lac, we should start considering if his actions are of good deeds, if he is practicing as APPROPRIATELY as the Buddha taught Subhada, and if he

disseminates the Dharma as the Buddha had taught Subhada. If the answers are yes, we can conclude that he is doing good deeds. As he, a practitioner, is practicing methods which Buddha taught to Subhada, this world would soon have an Arhat who achieves Enlightenment. Don't you think so, too?

(3) **Proper Speech:** When we know things thoroughly, we must present them correctly without twisting or covering them, just like we show a photograph. If it is white or black, dirty or clean, we must say as it is. We do not need to mince our words to please listeners. While trying to please listeners, we are telling lies. Even though they are white lies, they are still lies!

(4) **Proper Action:** Mahayana monks wrongly explain this method as WORK or JOB or CAREER. Proper Action means that all actions that we conduct through our

body, speech, and thinking must not lead to unwholesome or destructive consequences. All our actions, speeches and thoughts must be good. We must be aware that our SPEECH CAN ACT AS A HAMMER, and that our speeches can cause widespread storms and wars!

(5) **Proper Livelihood:** Don't live our life at the cost of others. That means we must not torture others, not kill other living beings and not eat animal flesh.

(6) **Proper Effort**: We should always, constantly and continuously make efforts in practicing the Dharma until we achieve our goal (Enlightenment). Our mind has been gradually influenced by evil and unwholesomeness since our birth until the time we decide to start practicing the Buddha Dharma. Thus, we must keep making efforts to practice the True Buddha Dharma to gradually get rid of the evil influences

and to cultivate our mind with good deeds and wholesomeness. As good deeds and wholesomeness blossom within us, we also have mastered our mind.

(7) **Proper Mindfulness:** This does not mean "reciting mantra" as wrongly explained by Mahayana monks! This means one practices mindfulness by choosing (the virtues and lifestyle of) the Buddha, His Dharma, holy monks, or Buddhist Precept (Buddhist principles of morality). PICK ONLY ONE (of those) as your objective, always bear the objective in your foremost mind as the guidance to your practice. We should practice living like the Buddha or holy monks did. We should practice as per instructions in the True Buddha Dharma. We follow Buddhist moral principles. As we practice until our mind is perfected (with those values), we will surely achieve Enlightenment.

(8) **Proper Concentration:** We should always, constantly and continuously remind and incline our mind toward the True Buddha Dharma without distraction. Especially once the practitioner is able to attain and maintain the states of the Four Dhyanas - the Four Noble Meditational Concentrations, he or she should ardently pursue the realization of the Transcendental Threefold Knowledge with which the practitioner would become DEFILEMENT-FREE, and completely obliterate all his/her affliction and suffering. Thus, he or she becomes an Arhat.

3) 12 Linked-chain dependent originations

As the Buddha was teaching, a man came to ask him:

Honorable Gotama, is it true that I make myself suffer?

- That's not true.

Is it true that other people cause my sufferings?

- That's not true.

Is it true that we make me suffer?

- That's not true.

The man got upset and harshly asked:

Honorable Gotama, then who create my sufferings?

- It is the 12 linked-chain dependent originations that make you suffer! One origination leads to the other. When an origination is abolished, others are also extinguished. The 12 linked-chain dependent originations include:

➢ **Unknowing:** Desires and urges

➢ **Action**: Because of desires and urges, we conduct greedy and sexual acts.

➢ **Consciousness**: Due to sexual desire, consciousness is created.

➢ **Form**: Forms exist with six senses, including eye, ear, nose, mouth, body and mind.

➢ **Six Entrances**: The six senses are gateways through which six objects (of these senses) enter our body. For instance, our eyes see the moon; Our legs and arms play ball; Our mouth drinks water. Things outside our body are objects.

➢ **Contact**: Because we have the six senses, we contact the six objects.

➢ **Feeling & sensation**: As we contact the six objects, we have feelings, including pain, pleasure, bitterness, sadness, joyfulness, etc.

➢ **Affection**: After we contact the six objects, we come to like or love some certain things.

➢ **Grasping:** Because we like or love some things, we try to grasp them.

➢ **Owning**: We tightly keep and own things that we like.

➢ **Birth / Life:** Things that we keep and own are belong to us, including our lover, our wife, our children, our house, our garden, our field, our country, our religion, our pagoda and our body. All of them are fetter of fondness.

➢ **Sufferings:** Because we own things, we have to protect and develop them, which cause our worries and fears.... So, WE CREATE OUR OWN SUFFERINGS.

4) 37 Aids conducing to enlightenment

These are 37 methods aimed to assist our practice until we achieve Enlightenment. They are categorized into groups of four aids, five aids and seven aids. However, it would suffice that we practice only one method until perfection. Other qualities of the same group will be automatically developed accordingly. For instance, among greed, anger, delusion, arrogance and doubt, we only need to get rid of one of them, such as greed or anger. That should be sufficient, (because) once we eliminate our greed or our anger, the other four issues (in this group of five) also disappear.

➢ **5 intellectual capacities** of faith, endeavor, mindfulness, meditation, and wisdom.

o The capacity of faith is the root of believing.

o The capacity of effort enables us to continuously practice the Buddha Dharma without interruptions.

o The capacity of mindfulness enables us to practice and conform to Buddhist disciplines without any violations, even the small mistakes, just like the Buddha and holy monks.

o The capacity of meditation enables us to stop our six senses from chasing six objects.

o The capacity of wisdom enables us to gain knowledge of the Truths (therefore liberation). With knowledge of the Truths, we are no longer bound to mundane knowledge and institutionalization. With WISDOM, ignorance disappears.

➢ **5 powers** of faith, effort, mindfulness, meditation, and wisdom are achieved when we successfully execute these five intellectual capacities mentioned above through practicing the True Buddha Dharma. Once the five intellectual capacities matured, these superpowers begin to show!

➢ **4 Right efforts:** the practitioner should focus on preventing and abolishing evil deeds and experiences through BODY, FEELINGS/

SENSATIONS, MIND, AND PHENOMENA. (prevent, abolish unwholesomeness, rise and cultivate wholesomeness)

➢ **4 immeasurable minds:** the practitioner should cultivate the immeasurable loving kindness, compassion, joy, and relinquishment to perfection. These immeasurables should aim toward (and for) the practitioner, not to others.

➢ **4 unfailing purities:** the practitioner picks either the Buddha, holy monks, Buddhadharma, or the Buddhist principles of morality as his or her practice paradigm and cultivate until the values (of the model) became intrinsic. Please note that no prayers, or begging involved here. How can we beg the Buddha Dharma or the Buddhist disciplines to help us?

➢ **4 fields of mindfulness:** We should be mindful of our body, feelings or sensations, mind, and phenomena in order to sweep all evil deeds and experiences out of these fields, wholesome deeds therefore will gradually pervade our mind.

➢ **7 (associated) aspects of Enlightenment:** When we practice the True Buddha Dharma until perfection, 7 aspects of Enlightenment will automatically appear in our body and mind.

➢ **4 Sufficiencies of the Will (or At-Will Powers):** When the seven aspects of Enlightenment appear, we can then use them for long duration throughout our practices of the Dharma, the four kinds of Sufficiency would emerge. With the four Sufficiencies, we can enter FOUR HOLY MEDITATIONAL STATUS at will. By directing our attention and mindfully command our body, our four Sufficiencies would execute accordingly at our will, shut off our six sense organs' activities, and enter a specific meditational state that we commanded. And also with these four Sufficiencies, we are able to reactivate our six sense organs at will and get back to normal state.

ATTENTION:

You should read this chapter just to be aware of those concepts. You should not dig deeply into their details. When you decide to practice the True Buddha Dharma, you should read further the Nikaya scriptures or books written by Venerable Thong Lac. If you dig deeply in theories, you are immersed back into the indulgence of trying sate your hunger for knowledge, another kind of desire. As you are immersed in the quest of satisfying your hunger for knowledge, you have lost into the practices of evil deeds! Just a minor mistake can lead to the whole wrongness, like a derailed train. A miss is as good as a mile!

5) 5 Aggregates or Processes

A human mind has five important "departments" or processes whose operation we need to know about in order to thoroughly understand ourselves. With knowledge of the operation of those processes we can correctly practice the True Buddha Dharma. Our body has heart, liver, stomach, lungs and brain. We also know many things exist even without seeing them, such as craving, anger, delusion, pride and doubt. There are things known by the Buddha only. The Buddha taught us about the five aggregates or processes within the body. Even modern science has not recognized the five aggregates. This is a specific knowledge of Buddhism only taught to the Bhiksus by the Buddha. After Ananda, the last Arhat passed away, no one else know about the operation of the five aggregates. Although Arhats noted about the five aggregates in the Nikaya scriptures, all monks and scholars in the world do not understand what exactly the five aggregates are and how they operate. What they've been trying to expound in regards of those aggregates are purely speculation and conjecture. Only until our time did Arhat Thich Thong Lac appeared and clearly explained to us about the five aggregates. And now, Bhiksu Thanh Thien further explains them by using conventional languages to help monks, nuns and Buddhist laypeople in Vietnam understand about the operation of the five aggregates. Monks, nuns and Buddhist laypeople please note that ONLY ARHATS CAN EXPLAIN CLEARLY THE OPERATION OF THE FIVE AGGREGATES. Then Venerable Thong Lac was an Arhat, wasn't he? While monks, nuns and lecturers at Buddhism universities in the world do not understand ANYTHING about the five aggregates and how they operate, all monks, nuns and Buddhist laypeople in Vietnam now understand them. Let's pay our sincere reverence and gratefulness to Arhat Thich Thong Lac who enlightened us.

(1) Before practicing the True Buddha Dharma, we need to understand what the five aggregates are, particularly the Subconscious Mind. Only with a thorough knowledge about the operation of the Subconscious Mind could we practice the True Buddha Dharma successfully. Our body and mind comprised of the five aggregates: Conscious Mind, Sensation, Subconscious Mind, Operation Mechanism and Enlightening Consciousness. Of course, our physical body is created from water, fire, earth and air. When we die, our body will be converted back into those original basic elements!

➢ **Conscious Mind:** The center of our cognitive awareness.

➢ **Sensation:** The faculty of feelings and

sensations such as pain, pleasure, sadness, joy, bitterness

- **Subconscious Mind:** The center of our subconsciousness. Its operation is beyond space and time. We often dream during our sleep, that is an activity of our subconscious mind! Or when we wonder about something, for instance: thinking about what our relatives are doing in a distant place. That's when our subconscious mind is operating.

- **Operation/Operating Mechanism:** After we decide what to do, the Operation Mechanism drives the actions as per our decision. For instance, we want to eat then we eat, we want to sleep then we go to sleep, we want to debate then we debate. The Operation Mechanism, like a servant, works as per directions!

- **Enlightening Consciousness:** This operational center stays inactive until we achieve the three kinds of clarity (The Threefold Knowledge) through practicing the True Buddha Dharma, the three kinds of clarity will direct our mind. Once this operational center is active, its operation is beyond space and time. The Enlightening Consciousness is stronger than the Subconscious Mind, thus it can control the Subconscious Mind.

(2) Monks, nuns and Buddhist followers in Vietnam should be proud of having Arhat Thich Thong Lac who explained to us about the ENLIGHTENING CONSCIOUSNESS. Although Venerable Minh Chau has translated the Nikaya Scriptures into Vietnamese, he couldn't clearly understand the operation of the five aggregates, particularly the ENLIGHTENING CONSCIOUSNESS. Only Arhats can understand this. Why do only Arhats understand the ENLIGHTENING CONSCIOUSNESS? Because only Arhats have the Threefold Knowledge - insights to control

the operation of the subconscious mind. It is clear, isn't it? We should be proud that we now have a chance to be enlightened by Arhat Thich Thong Lac through the knowledge of the operation of the five aggregates which were taught by the Buddha to His disciples!

(3) Jesus, Amitabha Buddha, Maitreya Buddha, Gods, none of them understand - and therefore can't teach us - the operation of the five aggregates. This proves that they are FAKE! It is Arhat Thich Thong Lac who is the REAL DEAL, real holy monk!

(4) Let's pretend that we were kings or queens, our conscious mind would be our trustworthy courtier who always has wholesome tendencies and help us to have a better life. It is a Righteous Path.

The subconscious mind is a sycophantic courtier who always wants to us to satisfy our hungers for pleasures, so that our body and mind sink deeply into enchantments and ecstasys! It is Evil.

Between the Conscious Mind and the Subconscious Mind is the HEART. Whether the HEART, like our child, heads to the Righteous Path or the Evil Path, we (have no choice but to) follow it.

(5) We need to understand that the Conscious Mind wanders (and can't focus) until we grow up and become an adult. Only then does the Conscious Mind starts functioning and helps us understand life issues, differentiate right and wrong, and get to know the Four Noble Truths. Meanwhile, the Subconscious Mind has started its operation since our birth. Moreover, the Subconscious Mind has 33 channels of subconsciousness, like seven notes (and octaves) in music (A, B, C, D, E, F, G) which can be used to compose an infinite quantity of songs. The Subconscious

Mind with 33 channels of subconsciousness are even more powerful. It gives us countless scenarios and imaginations to help us to perfectly sate our hunger for pleasures! Effectively, our HEART always follows the SUBCONSCIOUS MIND. That's why the Buddha taught us the method of CRITICAL THINKING ON WISE ATTENTION, so that we can use it as a rein to tame a wild horse. We are the same. We should cooperate with the Conscious Mind to use the Critical Thinking on Wise Attention to train the HEART to follow our orders. As we master our HEART, we will no longer succumb to temptations.

There are 33 different types (or characteristics) of psychic phenomena within our subconsciousness. They are:

1. Visual hallucination (images of the past or the future, images in dreams or in meditation... were generated by a frequency from our subconsciousness)

2. Auditory Hallucination (sounds generated by another frequency from our subconsciousness only heard by oneself or a group because of same ritual, practices, or same psychedelic drug they share)

3. Olfactory hallucination (similar experience like the ability to smell in dreams)

4. Gustatory hallucination (similar experience like the ability to taste food in dreams, or like when you see lime you start to drool)

5. Tactile hallucination (hallucinations felt by the sense of touch and feeling)

6. Keen eloquence (especially for manipulation)

7. Haphazard urges and thoughts

8. Subconsciousness of dreams

9. Subconsciousness of non-Buddhism's precepts

10. Subconsciousness of non-Buddhism's concentration

11. Subconsciousness of knowledge

12. Subconsciousness of eye (unexpected view without the eye-medium)

13. Subconsciousness of ear (unexpected hearing without the ear-medium)

14. Subconsciousness of nose (unexpected smell without the nose-medium)

15. Subconsciousness of tongue (unexpected taste without the tongue-medium)

16. Subconsciousness of body (unexpected feeling without the body-medium)

17. Subconsciousness of thoughts (unexpected thought without the intellect-medium)

18. Supernatural subconsciousness

of eye (ability to see from thousands miles apart)

19. Supernatural subconsciousness of ear (ability to hear from thousands of miles apart)

20. Supernatural subconsciousness of nose (ability to smell from thousands of miles apart)

21. Supernatural subconsciousness of tongue (ability to taste from thousands of miles apart)

22. Supernatural subconsciousness of body and feet (ability of transformation)

23. Supernatural subconsciousness of mind (ability to know past and future events)

24. (Meditational) Realm of boundless space

25. (Meditational) Realm of boundless consciousness

26. (Meditational) Realm of nothingness

27. (Meditational) Realm of Neither Subconsciousness nor Non-subconsciousness

28. Subconsciousness of qigong

29. Subconsciousness of inner force control

30. Subconsciousness of outer force control

31. Subconsciousness of human energy control

32. Subconsciousness of flying kungfu

33. Subconsciousness of horse stance kungfu

(6) Other religions and the fake Amitabha Buddha teach their followers that the HEART

means the physical HEART or what lies in the HEART. Bhiksu Thanh Thien affirms that what they teach is wrong. So, what is the HEART here? The HEART is like our child. Even when we grow old, our HEART remains childlike. When this child follows the Subconscious Mind, we fall into evil desires for pleasures. When this child follows the Conscious Mind, we become holy people. Where does the HEART stay? It wanders like a wild horse. When we are painful or joyful, the HEART stays in Sensation. When we are thinking, it stays in the Subconscious Mind. When we are considering/reflecting, it moves into the Conscious Mind. When we quarrel, fight or conflict with others, it moves into Operation aggregate. When we are sleeping, it rests in the Subconsciousness.

(7) As he finds out and clearly understands the operation of the HEART, like a mouse moving among the five aggregates, Bhiksu

Thanh Thien shares this knowledge to monks, nuns and Buddhist followers for their REFERENCE and CONSIDERATION. When we encounter things in the outer environment, it is the HEART that has the quickest reactions, then the Conscious Mind follows in helping us make decisions. For instance, a person come to fight us or quarrel with us, the HEART immediately REACTS in suggesting two actions: fight back or ignore; quarrel or ignore. Why are there these two suggestions? Immediate fighting back or quarrelling is a natural reaction. IGNORING comes from the HEART having been trained by practicing CRITICAL THINKING ON WISE ATTENTION! Please think about this. If Bhiksu Thanh Thien has to explain in more details, it will take the whole page! After the HEART reacts, the CONSCIOUS MIND appears to make decision on fighting/quarrelling or ignoring.

(8) It is necessary to understand that the

Conscious Mind, the trustworthy courtier, operates slowly, naively and orderly, which makes us annoyed and displeased. Meanwhile, the Subconscious Mind, the flattering servant, with 33 channels of subconsciousness always gives us various choices of pleasures and sensorial gratifications that we cannot refuse! Like kings, how can we refuse good wine, beautiful ladies, delicious food, luxurious outfits and all sorts of other pleasurable things? Yet, the Conscious Mind prevents us from enjoying them! Can't let the conscious mind stop us from enjoying the pleasures for now, even if we have to die! That's why we must know how to skillfully deploy the method of critical thinking on wise attention in order to drive the HEART away from the sways of temptations and to convince it to work hard in practicing the Buddha Dharma until achieving Enlightenment. Similarly, you can imagine a gambling addict playing hard and his wife who is trying to talk him out of gambling. The addict told his wife: "You can leave me but I will not quit gambling". A woman addicting gambling also says that I would rather leave my husband and children than quitting gambling.

By now, have practitioners understood the importance of critical thinking on wise attention in your practice of the True Buddha Dharma? Thanks to Venerable Thong Lac's tremendous effort in explaining the Buddha's teaching to us! Mahayana monks do not understand this method. They consider that it is a SELF-INSINUATION method! They do not know how to deploy the method correctly. Yet, they blame that Venerable Thong Lac teaches it wrongly. They do not know that they are so IGNORANT and so insolent to the holy Arhat Thich Thong Lac!

NOTE:

(1) Once we achieve Enlightenment, where does the HEART stay? By that time, the Critical Thinking on Wise Attention method has successfully tightened the HEART to the Conscious Mind. As the (will of the) HEART willingly and peacefully stays with the Conscious Mind, we can enter meditation to reach the Threefold Knowledge. Effectively, we can complete our practice of DISCIPLINE – MEDITATION – ENLIGHTENMENT and bring the ethics of KARMA-BASED HUMANISM to other people by teaching them ways to practice the True Buddha Dharma, so that they can also achieve Enlightenment.

(2) Why do quarrels happen among friends who are playing with one another or between wife and husband who are having a harmonic relationship?

-That is because our Subconscious Mind

is attacking us. Among the 33 channels of subconsciousness, when we stay in the same channels of subconsciousness, we have a harmonic relationship. When we stay in different channels, we fight each other. That's how it happens. So, we need to know the way the subconscious mind works. When we want to quarrel, IT IS BEST to go away or keep quiet and focus on deploying a command to drive away the desire of quarrelling. So that we can mitigate things and secure long-lasting happiness.

(3) Scholars work by incorporating their subconscious mind with their conscious mind because the subconscious mind operates beyond space and time, compared to the limited operation of the conscious mind. Children watch cartoons by their subconscious mind.

CONGRATULATIONS: Many Buddhist followers have sent appreciative emails to Bhiksu Thanh Thien, thanking him for his teaching which gives them a much better understanding in True Buddha Dharma! Bhiksu Thanh Thien feels truly happy because he feels that he has done a meaningful work to save others!

6) Practice one method, one-method practice

Trinh Thanh Hoai asked, on October 2, at 6.22am

Dear Bhiksu Thanh Thien,

I was in deep delusion and superstition. Thank to your teachings, I have been awakened. Thank you very much, thank you, thanks a lot to Bhiksu Thanh Thien. It is true as you teach that practicing the True Buddha Dharma is our own fight and triumph over ourselves...

Dear Bhiksu, I was deeply wrecked in addictions and delusions for many years. Now, thanks to Bhiksu Thanh Thien, I am awakened, yet I am still drowsy. How can I practice critical thinking on wise attention and the six basic practicing methods? Please teach me one practicing method which can help me to be fully awake and to catch on the right track of practicing as per your teachings. With my sincere thanks to you.

EXPLANATION

(1) Though this question arrived more than three months ago, Bhiksu Thanh Thien did not answer it until now. It was because Bhiksu Thanh Thien needed to experiment the methods before giving an answer. Similarly, before Bhiksu Thanh Thien taught practitioners about taking only one meal per day, he practiced walking meditation in long distance for six hours plus exercising for two

hours at the level of professional athletics, in total 8 hours per day (while he took only one meal each day). He continuously practiced at that intensity for 12 months and found that his health and mind were in good conditions. Only then did he start teaching and committing to guiding practitioners to practice taking one meal per day. Bhiksu Thanh Thien is the only bhiksu in the world who TEACHES TRUE BUDDHA DHARMA PRACTICES as per the Buddha's teachings and does not take disciples. Now as he has experimented the methods on himself, he starts teaching to monks, nuns and Buddhist laypeople.

(2) WHY DOES NOT BHIKSU THANH THIEN TAKE DISCIPLES?

It is because every Buddhist is a disciple of SHAKYAMUNI BUDDHA. Each person can execute Buddhist practices to liberate oneself. Bhiksu Thich Thanh Thien only guided monks, nuns and Buddhist laypeople to better understand the Buddha's teachings and to execute the practices AS PER THE BUDDHA' TEACHINGS. These teachings are not invented by Bhiksu Thanh Thien, then he could not take people who follow these teachings as his DISCIPLES. Bhiksu Thanh Thien does not create his own TEACHINGs or his own religion, nor does he teach any methods which are different from Shakyamuni Buddha's teachings. That's why he does not accept anyone as his disciples. Bhiksu Thanh Thien only guides practitioners to KNOW HOW TO PRACTICE AS PER SHAKYAMUNI BUDDHA'S TEACHINGS so that people can progress their practice, master their birth/life, oldness, sickness, death, and LIBERATE themselves from sufferings.

(3) To be precise, Bhiksu Thanh Thien should have presented himself as an OLDER FELLOW and called people NEWER

FELLOWS. My NEWER FELLOWS, please accept my SINCERE APOLOGY. From now on, I, the OLDER FELLOW, will be your guide and you, NEWER FELLOWS, will be learners. Please do not introduce yourselves as my disciples because all of us are disciples of Shakyamuni Buddha! Everyone is equal in the True Buddha Dharma. Instead, please call yourself a Buddhist follower, monk, nun or your name, and "I would like to ask 'you', the older fellow to explain...." Please correct your introduction and stop calling yourselves my disciples.

For example: Nun/newer fellow/Buddhist follower/Minh Thang would like to ask...

Once we know we are wrong, we should correct immediately. Please stop praying the senseless Amita Buddha. If you are already advised about the senseless Amita Buddha, yet you still pray that name, then you are a senseless person!

(4) THIS IS A UNIQUE PRACTICING METHOD of (the True Buddha Dharma) which Bhiksu Thanh Thien has just experimented. Anyone who practices it would achieve wonderful results. IT IS UNBELIEVABLE BUT TRUE. The method is:

1. Before sleeping, practitioners should sit or lie still and breathe slowly and calmly in 5 minutes.

2. When you want to sleep, keep thinking about the time you start sleeping and the time you wake up. For instance, you want to sleep at 10pm and wake up at 4am, you think: "Hoai, sleep now, and wake up at 4am". With consistency in sending the command (to your body and mind) for a certain period of time, your mind will AUTOMATICALLY adjust to wake you up on time. There is no need to WORRY. Remember to call out your name. Using an alarm clock can also be helpful.

3. Once you wake up, do not lie still, instead, get up immediately. Then you sit still and breathe slowly and calmly in 5 minutes. When you breathe, watch your philtrum, the area on your face between the nose and the upper lip. Only keep an eye on the area, do not focus your attention in the action. If you focus, you will suppress your mind, which will lead to headache and facial tension. Just keep watching the area until you are accustomed to the action, then your mind will automatically enter an attention stage without your notice. You will then feel calm, relaxed and comfortable.

4. Once your mind is familiar with this practice for 5 minutes, you can extent the practice time DEPENDING on each individual. If you can extent the practice time to half an hour, it would be great.

5. After three months practicing the

method, you will feel your body relaxed, pleased and light. Your mind will become sharper and more alert. Your personality will become gentler and more lovable. HOW STRANGE IS THAT! At the same time, you will no longer be afraid of diseases.

6. This practicing method is helpful for anyone. Practitioners would no longer suffer from STRESS or ANXIETY. Particularly, students can learn lessons more easily and NO LONGER FEEL STRESSED or ANXIOUS during exams. Due to stress and anxiety, many students are very likely to forget lessons and knowledge that they've learned, therefore exam failure which leads to depression and suicide attempt to seek salvation in Amita Buddha of the imaginary ULTIMATE BLISS WESTERN LAND! This method also helps athletes and footballers to PREVENT SHORTNESS OF BREATH while they are competing for TROPHY.

7) Long distance walking meditation

MASTER, PLEASE TEACH ME WALKING MEDITATION IN LONG DISTANCE.

Indeed, long distance walking meditation sounds easy, yet most people practice this method wrongly! And many Buddhist laypeople have asked me about this method. I need to find a way to clearly explain this method so that everyone can understand it. That's why I delay the explanation until now. Buddhist laypeople who asked me about this method long time ago, please excuse me and don't be disappointed!

(1) Walk at your normal speed. If you usually walk fast, then walk fast. If you usually walk slowly, walk slowly. You just walk at your own pace as per your own routine. But you must be relaxed, at ease, gentle and comfortable while walking.

(2) During your ordinary routine walk,

you normally watch the surroundings and look at people. With walking meditation, however, you should look at your walking feet. Just keep an eye on your feet, do not lower your head which makes you tired. You should look ahead from time to time.

(3) During your walking meditation, keep thinking:

1. Walk firmly (in order) to strengthen my legs and soften the ground, walk (in order) to stabilize my mind and achieve enlightenment, meditate on leaving greed, anger and delusion.

2. Walk for a while then command your mind on wise attention such as: "be as clean as a washed conch shell! (Free from all attachments)" or "(the mind must) leave greed, anger and delusion."

3. Walk for a while then send commands to clear or get rid of certain attachments out of the mind, such as: "emotions, feelings, and

sensations are impermanent", or "sensual desires must leave this mind and body!", or contemplate on leaving greed, anger and delusion.

4. Walk for a while then send commands and focus to treating diseases in your body. For example, if you are suffering from headaches, you should repeat the thinking: "These feelings and sensations are impermanent, this headache must leave my body, and I am abandoning greed, anger and delusion." These statements of wise commands should suffice for one session of walking meditation.

(4) Keep walking and repeating the thoughts. Once the practice has been familiarized, you can walk for a very long time without feeling tired and noticing time passing by.

(5) What are the benefits of the practice?

1. Prevent sleepiness

2. Diminish laziness

3. Increase determination and inspiration in practicing the True Buddha Dharma.

4. Improve health

5. Enhance skillfulness in critical thinking and commanding on wise attention

6. Time was wisely used

7. RANDOM THOUGHTS WERE ANNIHILATED.

(6) The annihilation of random thoughts is the key and foundation for us to comfortably practice breathing meditation, mindfulness, relinquishment (of the attempts of the mind), mind guiding, mind taming, and leaving pleasure and evil deeds. It is because all those practices result in preventing arising thoughts, so that we can easily enter deeper meditational states later.

(7) What are other benefits of long-distance walking meditation? With consistency in walking meditation, paying wise attention, and sending wise commands to the mind and body, at some point the (sick) practitioner will inadvertently find that his illnesses are gone!

(8) With True Buddha Dharma practice, the practitioner must cultivate for himself an ASPIRATION in practicing the Dharma. Unlike practice methods often taught by Mahayana monks, which are often A HYPOCRITICAL PRETENSE, A PLAY, A MASQUERADE in SLUGGISH MOTION. In Mahayana walking meditation, practitioners often walk very gingerly and slowly (suppressing their mind), and act with solemnity and modesty (suppressing their mind). They always notice if people are observing them, which means that they have to put on their act in public due to fears of being wrong and being

discovered. They need to persuade those who watch them that they were practicing Buddha Dharma. They merely perform rather than actually practice the True Buddha Dharma. They practice in delusion which makes them become SLUGGISH.

(9) When it comes to practicing True Buddha Dharma, our mannerism ought to be strong and comfortable. One must also be an inspired practitioner, highly motivated, and pay attention to no one else. For instance, when we first practice the six basic methods, the sessions are so short that we (often) feel bored and disappointed. In such case, we should close the door, stand on tippy toe, and jump up and down to create an energetic spirit in order to be ready to fight against our hunger for pleasures. Remember not to jump or walk too much. Just gradually increase your practice time. Besides, as for the six basic methods, practicing sessions for beginners

can be too short to some people, we can certainly add one, two or three extra sessions whenever it is suitable to our schedule. We should practice our critical thinking and commanding on wise attention as if we are singing a song.

(10) Throughout our walking meditation, we do not greet or talk to other people because we do not look around.

(11) MAGNIFICENT RESULTS WILL HAPPEN! When we are in serious diseases or on the verge of death, we will attain NATURAL REACTIONS in our body that makes us feel utterly composed!

8) Critical thinking on wise attention - mind training with sustained thought

What is Critical thinking on wise attention or Mind Training with sustained thought? It means using direct and succinct statement to address intentions - wise and constructive - that we want our mind to be accustomed to. We constantly, always and persistently repeat the statement(s) until our mind is familiar with them, then our mind will follow our orders. For example: because we are used to eating animal flesh, when we change to vegetarianism, we will feel irritated, dizzy, uncomfortable, quick to get hungry, weak and anxious. We should always repeat the sentences: "I should become a vegetarian. Eating animal flesh is too cruel and disgusting!" and cultivate that thought until our mind is imbued with the idea, then we execute vegetarianism. We will then find that vegetarian food delicious and we no longer want to eat meat. When we are used to vegetarianism, we will feel disgusted and sick when we see people chewing animal flesh. We will feel creepy and want to go away! Remember that we must repeat the wise notions that we want to cultivate until our mind is familiar with them before we start executing.

(1) Why must we train the Mind/Heart to be familiar with the ideas? Because our Mind/Heart is similar to a child. We often pamper it by satisfying its desires. The Heart often follows our SUBCONSCIOUSNESS because the subconsciousness has attracted the Mind/Heart since our birth. As a result, the Mind/Heart is used to chasing after pleasures. As we grow up, our conscious mind has matured. We have read the Four Noble Truths. We have understood that our life is transitory, filled with sufferings of birth, oldness, sickness and death. We decide to practice the True Buddha Dharma to overcome the sufferings. We must reduce our hunger for pleasure. If we want to reduce our hunger for pleasure, we must train our mind/heart to gradually leave the hunger, meaning leaving the SUBCONSCIOUS MIND's influences. If we want our Mind/Heart to

gradually separate from the SUBCONSCIOUS MIND, we must constantly, always and persistently remind the Mind/Heart with words of good faith. Due to the words of good faith, our Mind/Heart will slowly get rid of the SUBCONSCIOUS MIND's influence and become connected with the CONSCIOUS MIND.

(2) How can we know if the reminders are effective to our Mind/Heart? We can observe an experiment with two children. A mom told her child that: "Remember not to fight back when schoolmates attack you. Instead, you should report the attack to your teacher who will then punish the attackers." The child remembered the mom's words. When a schoolmate attacked her, she quietly went to her teacher to report. Another mom told her child: "Whenever a child annoys you, fight back immediately. Don't be afraid. I've got your back!" Then the child remembered the words and fought back another child who annoyed

him the day after. This is an evidence that the children learnt by heart whatever their moms said. Learning by heart means reminding our Mind/Heart. Once ideas are implanted in our Mind/Heart, the Mind/Heart will drive us to react accordingly whenever we are in similar situations. That is because our Mind/Heart is always the first function among others to react to any contacts from outside to our mind or our body. THE IMMEDIATE REACTION OF FIGHTING BACK COMES FROM THE MIND/HEART WITH HABIT OR PRE-IMPLANTED REMINDERS. Then the conscious mind and the subconscious mind intervene to implement solutions for current problems.

(3) In order to understand thoroughly the influence/effect (of this practice) for ourselves:

a) We (for example) constantly repeat: "Turn big problems into small ones and small problems into nothing". Once our Mind/ Heart is familiar with the thinking, we will not fight back when someone causes troubles to us. Instead, we would calmly ask: "What's problem?" When we clearly understand the problem, through our conscious mind, we act wonderfully. As a result, all problems are solved, and all things are put in order perfectly.

b) Another example, upon hearing that your husband conducts adultery, you boil the thinking that: "When you come back home, you will taste my wrath. I will surely beat you up." Then once your husband gets through the door, you immediately attack him. Thus, domestic violence occurs!

c) On the contrary, if you repeat the thinking: "It is normal that men are attracted to girls! As long as he's willing to come home, I should let it go." When your husband gets home, you pleasantly talk with him and do not immediately mention his adultery misconduct. Your family will maintain its harmony and happiness.

(4) You should use short commands that work with your mentality and personality. You should never imitate someone else's command. Even though that command sentence sounds good, it is good for that particular person, but not for you. You should invent your own commands that your Mind/ Heart finds easy to get familiar with. Maybe you command the same ideas but different wordings. We should wisely choose wordings which work with our own Mind/Heart, so that our Mind/Heart can quickly learn and remember them. For example, if your Mind/ Heart is more compatible with soap opera genre, it will not accept strong, boot-camp-like commands which forces your attention. Don't you think so?

(5) Practicing critical thinking on wise attention includes three components:

a) Long-term reminding (of the wise attention). Venerable Thong Lac kept repeating the sentence: "The Mind is as clean as a washed conch shell. The Mind must leave greed, anger and delusion". Why must we constantly and persistently practice critical thinking and commanding our mind on wise attention? The long-term practice aims to help our Mind/Heart to renounce all temptations. We will face many temptations while practicing Buddha Dharma. Because we practice critical thinking and commanding our mind/heart on wise attention over long period, our Mind/Heart becomes familiar with the thoughts and easily neglects temptations whenever they emerge, despite how attractive they are. What might happen if we do not practice constantly and persistently? Our Mind will have choices when facing temptations. If the temptations are so attractive, we cannot reject them; ergo, all our progress will be ruined instantly. That's why you must not imitate anyone else's command sentences. You should create your own statements that works with your personality.

b) Short-term practice in order to solve our issues one by one. For instance, we cultivate our attention to giving up eating animal flesh and turning to vegetarianism. When we are used to and at ease with vegetarianism, we can turn our attention to reducing the number of meals that we take each day, one by one, until we can live with only one meal per day. The next wise attention that we want to cultivate is totally up to us. After successfully taking only one meal per day, Bhiksu Thanh Thien constantly commanded: "Sensual desires must leave my mind and body. (The mind/heart must) leave greed, anger and delusion." It took him over three years to achieve success in this practice!

c) Momentary practice of sending commands on wise attention to address sudden or momentary issues. For instance, the subconscious mind unexpectedly triggers homesickness and urges us to return home. We should immediately command our mind on wise attention to drive the emerging thinking away: "No way. Do not go anywhere." Make your voice strong, then we can instantly dismiss the urge. Or when we feel hungry, we promptly send a command to our mind: "Not now. Not yet time (for meal)!" ...

(6) In order to find peace for our mind when parting from our loved ones, Bhiksu Thanh Thien found a gentle, comfortable, and easy preemptive method to be practiced beforehand for both the farewell-or and farewell-ee to achieve inner-peace in time of separation, free from separation anxiety. The method is to use wise reminders and commands to gradually train us with the

six basic methods. During the practice, the farewell-ee would naturally feel upcoming separations with the farewell-or. Over time, we will become at peace with the separation anxiety. When we practice the method successfully, we can handle separations in peace. Stayers will encourage leavers to go in peace and leavers will enthusiastically depart with confidence in their quest of self-defeat. That is because we have overcome challenges of worry, fear, doubt and anxiety. We are no longer afraid of sadness and longing, or worried by hunger and thirst. A hermitage for solitude practice now becomes heaven for us to enthusiastically fight against the marauders of the realm of samsara. This is pretty clear and straightforward, don't you think? This is a method that Bhiksu Thanh Thien has practiced with success and now shares with other practitioners! If he did not practice the True Buddha Dharma successfully, he would not know all these to share to us. The most wonderful art of farewell is that the farewell-ee has sufficient time to prepare his/her own attitude and that leaver has all of his/her belongings ready. Therefore, there will be no separation anxiety!

ROMANCE & FAMILY FONDNESS is the most entrenched and difficult thing for us to get rid of. Once we have peacefully cut off our fondness, we also have successfully put our 2 feet onto the boat for the True Buddha Dharma journey, figuratively speaking.

(7) Don't ever be mistaken that we must complete repaying our secular debts before we start practicing the True Buddha Dharma. Those debts will never be completely repaid. The Buddha taught us that if we stop, we will sink; if we move forward, we will drift; the only way for us is to surmount. That means if we stay still, we will sink in the flow of desires

for pleasures; if we move forward, we will drift away in the flow of desires for pleasures. Only by practicing the True Buddha Dharma, can we surmount the flow of desires for pleasures to secure our control over birth, oldness, sickness and death and to escape from the rebirth cycle of suffering, samsara. That also means we have fully repaid all our debts of secular life! That's why when we decide to practice the True Buddha Dharma, we should separate from husband and children. Each person has his/her own way of life and death which we should not worry about. They may even have a better life without us, if their way of life is good! If their destiny is a hard life, that is their own karma that they must suffer! If we continue to linger and worry about them, we should not practice the True Buddha Dharma. We should not arrange anything for them. It is better that we just let their life happens as it is ought to be.

(8) How can we prevent sleepiness and laziness? In his experience, Bhiksu Thanh Thien practices long distance walking meditation for six hours each day. After three months, he naturally became energetic and enthusiastic in practicing the True Buddha Dharma and no longer felt sleepy. In his first week, he practiced long distance walking meditation for one hour. He increased the practice time to two hours in the second week, four hours in the third week and six hours in the fifth week. There is a question that why Venerable Thong Lac's teachings on dealing with sleepiness and laziness are different from those of Bhiksu Thanh Thien. Because Venerable Thong Lac taught practitioners who already have some experience in practicing Buddha Dharma. Bhiksu Thanh Thien, meanwhile, guided beginners who are trying to get used to the methods. Once we are familiar with the Buddha Dharma's methods, our practice will become easier.

(9) How can we prevent hunger before meal time? We feel hungry before meal time because our subconscious mind pre-programmed it that way, we are in fact not truly hungry, yet. That's why before meal time, we should practice long distance walking meditation or do something and we should only have meal at the right time. After repeating this practice a few times, our mind will be familiar with it and we no longer feel hungry before meal time. After we are used to this practice, it is wonderful that we do not feel hunger even after meal time. A strange phenomenon is that we would feel full all the time after meals and the idea of eating something never crosses our mind, even when foods are in front of us!

(10) How can we practice solitude without being emotionally fluctuated by thoughts arisen from our subconscious mind? Focus on practicing the six basic methods and the

one method that we chose to practice. When we abide in the awareness of our body and mental states, we will forget the surrounding altogether, and time passing us by quietly and calmly. If a thought emerges, we will immediately state a command directly to our mind to drive it away.

(11) Is it healthy and manageable for us to take one meal per day? Bhiksu Thanh Thien examined the idea by exercising in a fitness center and outside at the intensity level of professional athletics for over 12 months (while taking one meal per day) and he found himself still healthy and untroubled. Since then, he ensures that taking one meal per day works for manual workers, and they can even save money (from not taking unnecessary meals) for other things. Moreover, with only one meal per day, our sexual desire will gradually be dissipated and we will feel wonderful and peaceful!

(12) How can we prevent back hunching habit and back pain? By constantly practicing walking with our straight back and sitting with the back straightened upright like doing an exercise. When we are familiar with the practices, we will find ourselves naturally strong and no longer suffering from back hunching and back pain. When he was 65 years old, Bhiksu Thanh Thien suffered from back pain and lethargy due to his history of being a sexual maniac! By his 67, thank to Venerable Thong Lac who enlightened him on the TRUE BUDDHA DHARMA, Bhiksu Thanh Thien was determined to practice method as mentioned above. After 4 months, Bhiksu Thanh Thien has become exceptionally healthy and no longer suffered from any pain. At bedtime, he sends commands to put to sleep and to wake up at the time he wants; he will then fall asleep and wake up on time. It is magnificent and UNBELIEVABLE, but it's

true! When sending commands to your mind, remember to call out your name, so that our Mind will remember and act accordingly. If we call other name, our Mind will not act as per our commands!

(13) How to treat insomnia? By sending command to our mind the time to go to sleep and the time to wake up at our bedtime. When our mind is familiar with the idea and works as per the commands, we can go to sleep and wake up at the times we want.

(14) Our mind is not a God, how does it know the time to wake itself? It is too good to be true, right? There's no magic or superpower here. Our Mind does not know time, but with training, it can get used to the TIMING. Due to our constant practice of sending commands on wise attention to our Mind, the Mind is accustomed to the commands and act accordingly. Following the True Buddha

Dharma means to execute it and to gain empirical experiences on our very body and mind. There is no God or magic here!

(15) How can we verify to see if the practice is truly effective? We can experiment by letting a 3-year-old kid start watching cartoons at 9pm and stop at 9:20pm. After a few times, we can observe that even though the kid does not know how to read time, he/she would turn the TV on at exactly 9pm and off at 9:20pm despite the on-going cartoon. This experiment proves that his/her Mind works as per habit.

(16) We have been poisoned for over 2500 years by the misperception of Mahayana teaching to rely on our prayers. Now as we meet with the True Buddha Dharma, a TOTALLY NEW and STRANGE concept, we must have been very surprised and bewildered like newborn deer making its

first steps out to nature. That's why we need to slowly and gradually practice our Mind to make it get used to the Dharma and step by step drive unwholesome, deviant deeds away from our body and mind. Don't rush! Our Mind/Heart is like a child. We must practice it bit by bit, PRACTICE IN COMBINATION WITH RELAXATION so that our Mind and Heart can get used to the practice. If we rush and push, our Mind and Heart will be SUPPRESSED which would make us feel anxious, easily irritated, and quit the practice altogether.

Bhiksu Thanh Thien's advice to novice practitioners is to practice any Buddhist method in gradual fashion. When the practitioner becomes familiar with the practice, he can bit by bit brushes off deep-seated lust and desires out of his body and mind. Once unwholesome states are expunged, good and wholesome states will gradually grow and permeate our Mind. That means we can indeed control our Mind. That's when we totally defeat our own desires!

NOTE:

Do practitioners know why you have failed in practicing the True Buddha Dharma? Because you have been TOO EXCITED AND TOO EAGER, which inevitably leads to mind suppression - repressing lusts and desires from emerging. When your Mind is suppressed, you will want to fight back. The more you fight back, the more desperate you become! That's why practicing the True Buddha Dharma must proceed gradually, bit by bit. Don't worry about time. Don't care about what might come. Apply sustained thought and send command on wise attention to practice the six basic methods. When you become fluent in conducting the six basic methods, you can begin the saintly journey of fighting against the army of samsara's raiders with confidence and grace - a gentle fight yet a splendid triumph!

9) Practicing the six basic methods

Dear monks, nuns, and Buddhist laypeople who esteem Venerable Thich Thong Lac,

When you esteem Venerable Thong Lac, you must have acknowledged that He has enlightened us on THE TRUE BUDDHA DHARMA and brought us hope in practicing the Dharma, so that we can master birth, oldness, sickness and death and free ourselves from the miserable rebirth circle. Bhiksu Thich Thanh Thien is one of the Venerable's disciples. Thank to the Venerable's enlightening teachings, Bhiksu Thanh Thien has practiced the True Buddha Dharma with successes. Now Bhiksu Thanh Thien shares knowledge and experience gained from his practice of the True Buddha Dharma to you, so that you also understand the Truth which Arhat Thich Thong Lac disseminated to the public. Bhiksu Thanh Thien only shares his successfully attained knowledge and experiences. Bhiksu Thanh Thien never discusses aimless and useless theories nor does he talk about things that he has not experimented nor achieved through his own practice, which would only waste your time.

Firstly, you should recognize that the world during the Buddha's era was totally different from the current one. Effectively, depending on specific CONTEXTS, we should make SUITABLE ARRANGEMENTS in practicing Buddha Dharma. The most important point is that we still practice the True Buddha Dharma in harmony with the situations we are currently in. Nowadays, science and technology have exceptionally developed in order to serve human needs in all possible aspects. Besides, our parents and relatives have nurtured and pampered us by constantly fostering and indulging us with PLEASURES of the secular world. Inadvertently, our Mind and Heart have been deeply addicted to pleasures. Even though through (knowing) the FOUR NOBLE TRUTHS we understand that we need to practice the True Buddha Dharma to overcome sufferings in our life, we however cannot get rid of our habits of craving for PLEASURES. How can we practice the True Buddha Dharma successfully?

This is the crucial point that Bhiksu Thanh Thien has discovered through practicing the True Buddha Dharma properly and that he wants to share with you in order to help you SUCCEED in your practice.

Practitioners need to proceed with the six basic methods slowly until you are really proficient in these practices, including 1) Upright lotus position; 2) Solitary retreat;

3) Mindful breathing meditation; 4) Walking meditation; 5) Mind observation - sagacity meditation; 6) One meal per day.

Remember:

(1) Our purpose of practice is to train our Mind so that it is rewired and established with new habits. That's why we start out by practicing the methods with very short sessions and only gradually extend the practicing time when our Mind has become familiar and comfortable with the practice. Never rush in extending the practicing time too quickly, which will lead straight to failure. Since each practicing session is very short at the beginning, we can practice several times (throughout the day).

(2) We must practice at the exact time as planned. We must start and finish our practice at the exact time. For example, we plan to start practicing one method at 7pm and practice for

10 minutes. We must then start at 7pm and finish the practice after exactly 10 minutes. We must remember that we train our Mind to be accustomed to the practice.

(3) Before practicing any method, we must command our mind on a specific attention. Right after finishing our practice, we must also send commands to our mind. Commanding our mind/heart on wise attention means training our Mind/Heart to be accustomed to our commands. By perfecting our critical thinking and commanding on wise attention, we can control our Mind (and lead our Heart). That means we practice step by step to gain full control of our Mind and Heart.

(4) We must practice daily, like doing exercise. We practice as if we play, without concern, worry or expectation. Just let the technique and wisdom naturally be instilled in our Mind and become an indispensable habit.

That means when practicing this technique/ method, we only focus on our body and examine what are happening and changing in our body and our mind at that moment. This is the key for practicing the True Buddha Dharma.

(5) There are two stages in practicing the technique:

A- GETTING USED TO EACH METHOD

1. Sitting cross-legged and upright in lotus position: beginners should sit for two minutes only. Aged people can lean against a wall while sitting. Remember to send a command to yourself: "Sit in upright lotus position, I know that I am sitting upright in lotus position. (The mind must) leave greed, anger and delusion." When we finish the practice, send commands to our mind: "Stop, I know that I am ending the practice. (The mind must) leave greed, anger and delusion." Those who know how to sit properly just sit as usual.

2. Practicing solitary retreat: Each time we should sit in a closed-door room for 10 minutes without talking, listening, knowing, seeing or thinking. We must ignore whatever happens outside, and command our mind on wise attention: "Practicing solitude; I know that I am practicing solitude. I am abandoning greed, anger and delusion." When the practice time ends, we command: "Stop. I know I am finishing the practice. I am abandoning greed, anger and delusion."

3. Mindful breathing meditation:

Choose one (of the 19) rubric of the mindful breathing meditation as explained in Venerable Thong Lac's book and practice it for 5 minutes. Send command to our mind: "Breathe, I know I am breathing, inhaling and exhaling. I am abandoning greed, anger and delusion", and quietly watching our breaths at the philtrum. When the practice time ends, we command "Stop, I know I am finishing the practice. The mind must leave greed, anger and delusion."

4. Choose 1 technique of walking meditation as explained in Venerable Thong Lac's book to practice for 10 minutes. Heed attention by commanding: "Walk, I know that I am walking. I am abandoning greed, anger and delusion." When we sit down, we command: "Sit down, I know that I am sitting down. The mind must leave greed, anger and delusion." When we sit still, we command: "Breathe, I know I am breathing, inhaling and exhaling." When we stand up, we command: "I know I am standing up". When we walk, we command: "I know I am walking." Remember to add "I am abandoning greed, anger and delusion" after each command.

5. Sagacity meditation: Sit still for one minute, our body does not move, our brain

does not think, and no thought emerges in our mind. We command: "Sagaciously observe the mind, I am practicing sagacity in observing the mind." When the practice time ends, we command: "Stop, I know I am finishing the practice."

6. Taking one meal per day: We only need to constantly and persistently send commands of wise attention - of why we must have only 1 meal a day - to our mind, so that our mind gradually gets used to the idea. When our mind is familiar with the idea, we start practicing reducing meals one by one until we can easily take only one meal per day. We command: "I am determined to take only one meal per day, others can take only one meal per day, I also can." REMEMBER, commanding our mind can easily become repetitive and boring, but we must execute because that practice reminds our mind to follow and remember our commands. When

our mind is used to our commands, we will surprisingly realize that "I HAVE MASTERED MY MIND"!

B- COMBINING MANY METHODS IN ROUTINE PRACTICES

After we have been proficient in the six basic methods, we then combine them into a set of our routine practices. After practicing one method, we should take a few minutes break. When we take breaks, we practice sagacity meditation. When we practice solitude, we also combine sitting in upright lotus position, mindful breathing meditation, walking meditation, and sagacity meditation. Each practitioner should customize his or her own combination depending on his/her situation and state of mind. We must start out with very short sessions, then gradually extend the practice time until it covers all of our time.

WHAT ARE BENEFITS OF PRACTICING THE SIX BASIC METHODS?

1. Our mind has been accustomed to living in hunger for pleasures and unwholesome deeds. Now we practice the six basic methods so that our mind can gradually abandon evil deeds and hungers for pleasures, and to learn to abide in good faith. That means we step by step abandon our craving for pleasures and evil deeds, and make our mind accustomed to the True Buddha Dharma so that, as taught by the Buddha, desires and evil deeds can no longer influence our ACTIONS, WORDS, AND THOUGHTS and therefore can no longer bring sufferings to us or other sentient beings.

2. Once we have become familiar with and proficient at the six basic methods, and when opportunity comes, we can then decide to proceed further into higher stages of the Buddha Dharma practices with our readiness and intrepidity. We will be neither afraid of loneliness during solitary retreats, nor troubled with food craving and hunger once we can take one meal per day. Affinities no longer linger because we have already practiced leaving them. As we have been familiar with the six basic methods, we can then combine them together with one method of our own choice in order to advance our practice of the True Buddha Dharma toward success.

3. Even if we cannot get rid of our affinities and cravings for pleasures, we should still calmly continue practicing the six basic methods as a kind of daily exercise for our NEAR-DEATH MOMENTS. By that time, we will achieve two big benefits:

a) Due to our familiarity with the Buddha Dharma, our body's and mind's natural reactions will lead us to enlightenment at the last moments of our life. Many practitioners during the Buddha's time achieved enlightenment at this stage.

b) Thanks to our efforts to NURTURE OUR MIND WITH GOOD DEEDS, we will be able to surmount (our negative karma) and will not be reincarnated as an animal. We will be reborn as a human with better upbringing and experiences. As taught by the Buddha, if we stop we will sink, if we move forward we will drift. Our only choice is to surmount, meaning that the only way to pay off or extricate from our karmic debts is to cultivate and hone our mind with morality and good deeds by the techniques truly taught by the Buddha.

DO NOT HAVE FEAR IN TAKING ONE MEAL PER DAY! Bhiksu Thanh Thien has experimented this by exercising at a fitness center for two hours every day at the intensity level of a professional athlete for one whole year while taking only meal per day. He has maintained good physical health, and peaceful, relaxed mind. He guarantees that working people can still take one meal per day with peace while having extra money for other things. Especially, when being used to taking one meal per day, we no longer CRAVE FOR SEX!

NOTE:

1. I urge Buddhist monks, nuns and laypeople to actively copy and share this teaching to your friends, give a hand in creating a movement of practicing the True Buddha Dharma by influencing and encouraging each other (with this booklet). People want to cultivate good deeds and morality but they lack motivation. Thus, we should create

mutual supports to motivate each other in practicing the True Buddha Dharma.

2. We should practice the True Buddha Dharma slowly step by step as if we teach our children to learn while they play. Don't worry or rush because that action would - constrain, therefore - SUPPRESS OUR MIND!

ART OF PRACTICING THE TRUE BUDDHA DHARMA

A LETTER FROM A LAY BUDDHIST

Dear Bhiksu Thanh Thien,

On reading your teachings, I am enlightened and get to know the True Buddha Dharma. I really want to practice the True Buddha Dharma to liberate my own life from sufferings, just like you. But unfortunately, I'm still stuck with family responsibilities. Dear Bhiksu Thanh Thien, what should I do? Please tell me what to do to gain peace for myself - free from guilt - while I proceed with practicing the True Buddha Dharma. Thank you very much.

ANSWER TO ALL:

I have taught that practitioners should continue calmly living as you have been living and keep taking care of your family and fulfilling your role as a mother, wife or husband. Practitioners only need to spend a bit of time and space each day, just like for doing daily exercise, to GET USED TO THE BUDDHIST PRACTICES FIRST. As you patiently and regularly practice the True Buddha Dharma, your family members will then begin to believe in the practice. As your family members get used to seeing you practicing the True Buddha Dharma, they will also gradually want to practice leaving evil deeds and liberating their own life from sufferings.

Effectively, practitioners HAVE DONE A GOOD DEED BY HELPING YOUR FAMILY MEMBERS gracefully find their way to the

True Buddha Dharma in order to liberate their life from sufferings. Once your mind is imbued with the True Buddha Dharma, all desires, affinities, and evil deeds will gradually leave our mind, which help practitioners advance your practice more easily, comfortably and peacefully.

That's how you have created NATURALLY POSITIVE INFLUENCES to your surroundings. The sweet happiness we taste for refusing to cause any suffering to ourselves, people, and other sentient beings will interweave with the joy of SELF-RESCUE and SELF-DEFEAT, and will bring (us and our influencees) closer to the shore of liberation, THE ANNIHILATION OF SUFFERING.

Bhiksu Thanh Thien

FOLLOWING BHIKSU THANH THIEN'S INSTRUCTIONS IN PRACTICING THE TRUE BUDDHA DHARMA HELPS ELIMINATE ALL QUESTIONS, WORRIES, FEARS AND WANDERS!

CRITICAL THINKING ON WISE ATTENTION AND THE SIX BASIC METHODS

At first glance, can anyone believe this is true? Everyone would think that Bhiksu Thanh Thien was ARROGANT AND LYING! Please keep your cool, Bhiksu Thanh Thien will clearly explain that this is a truth.

1) Inhabit the buddhist discipline

(1) Before the Buddha left the world, He told practitioners that: Take my discipline - moral principles - as your teacher. That means practitioners must not violate any discipline taught by the Buddha, even the slightest one, while practicing the Dharma.

(2) Arhat Thich Thong Lac taught: DISCIPLINE – MEDITATION – WISDOM. We must fulfill the disciplines before we proceed with meditation. But did the Venerable teach practitioners how to fulfill the disciplines?

Without clear instructions, practitioners always worry about how to conform to and how to not violate the disciplines. So, practitioners would spend hours memorizing the disciplines and focus on not to violate them. This constant worry is unnecessary and useless, which could only waste the practitioners' time. Listen:

a) Bhiksu Thanh Thien takes an example from secular world that would help practitioners to understand. Would a disciplined, diligent, hardworking and docile student violate school disciplines? Of course not!

b) Similarly, would a practitioner, who diligently practices the True Buddha Dharma, stays in solitude and refuses to socialize, violate any discipline of the Dharma?

c) Bhiksu Thanh Thien also explains clearly that disciplines will only be effective from the time a practitioner decides to enter a hermitage to practice the method of his choice. That means once he enters the hermitage, all his prior faults are of the past, despite how serious they are. Evidently, the fact that hunters, killers and fornicators, who met the Buddha, listened to the Buddha's teachings, understood and decided to practice the True Buddha Dharma, have achieved Enlightenment.

d) The Buddha taught that: IF WE STOP, WE WILL SINK; IF WE MOVE FORWARD, WE WILL DRIFT; THE ONLY WAY FOR US IS TO SURMOUNT. Only by practicing the True Buddha Dharma can we surmount karma. That means when we have achieved Enlightenment, all secular karmas are cleared.

It is pretty clear, isn't it? (If) a practitioner knows how to practice the True Buddha Dharma, chooses for himself a method (out of the Buddha's teaching) and hone his mind with this method until it is completely imbued with Buddha-like qualities. By then, practitioners' mind has become Buddha's mind and practitioners have achieved Enlightenment. As we can see here that the practitioners did not need to know Buddhist disciplines; yet still could peacefully and comfortably fulfill the disciplines, didn't they? Before practicing the True Buddha Dharma, however, practitioners only need to quickly scan through the disciplines, just to get to know them, but don't be too concerned about them!

2) Abandoning desires and evil deeds, and growing good deeds

(1) The Buddha taught us to abandon our desires and evil deeds in order to attain the first stage of meditation. But did the Buddha teach how to abandon desires and evil deeds?

(2) Arhat Thich Thong Lac taught practitioners that they must abandon desires and evil deeds, and must cultivate good deeds to become perfect one! But did the Venerable teach practitioners how to do so? He only suggested that the easiest method is (conducting) THE FOUR RIGHT EFFORTS.

a) Bhiksu Thanh Thien has a question for those practitioners and others who proudly state that the Venerable's teachings are clear and enough!

Could you please describe how you have practiced abandoning your desires and evil deeds? For sure, many people cannot respond clearly! They understand the teachings but they cannot practice them successfully. At most, they can only conjecture!

b) Anyone who practice critical thinking on wise attention and the six basic methods fluently will automatically abandon their desires and evil deeds and grow good deeds. Isn't it magnificent?

c) Why so? When we can take only one meal per day, we have automatically abandoned our desires. When we practice solitude and do not come to contact with external stimulations, our six senses will automatically focus on our mind, thus, become dispassionate with our desires and evil deeds.

d) It is clear that when desires and evil deeds naturally and automatically leave us, a vacancy (in our mind) is created for good deeds to grow. That aligns with the Venerable's teachings that we abandon our desires and evil deeds in order to gracefully enter the first stage of meditation. That also aligns with the Buddha's teachings. Is there anything else more magnificent?

(3) HOW TO COMPLETELY RELINQUISH (THE ATTEMPTS OF) THE MIND?

When Venerable Thong Lac accepted a practitioner, He told him/her to enter a hermitage to gradually and completely relinquish (the attempts of) the mind. Practitioner Thanh Thien stayed the hermitage and went crazy! He thought to himself: "The master told me to enter the hermitage to relinquish (the attempts of) the mind. Yet, the master did not teach me how to do so. I sit idly, completely baffled and clueless. I thought of this and that but still did not know how to relinquish (the attempts of) the mind! This mess drove me to drink! I had no clue where to find the master - who was in hiding, from assassination - to ask for instructions on how to conduct the practice."

Now Bhiksu Thanh Thien clearly explains to practitioners that:

Practicing relinquishment (of the attempts of the mind) is the abandonment of desires and evil deeds itself. The six basic methods that are taught by Bhiksu Thanh Thien can help practitioners AUTOMATICALLY relinquish (the attempts of) the mind gently and completely. When a practitioner practices solitary retreat, his six senses will be trained to not follow external stimulations, your mind will not be swayed! It is so clear, isn't it?

(4) HOW TO ABANDON GREED, ANGER, DELUSION, PRIDE AND DOUBT?

Many practitioners were puzzled by this. The Venerable told practitioners: It is not easy to leave greed, anger, delusion, pride and doubt. They hide somewhere. Practitioners must find them and bring them into light.

Very simple, with critical thinking on wise attention and the six basic methods, practitioners gradually bring the six senses' attention toward the mind and they no longer attached to the six sensory inputs. Therefore, greed, anger, delusion, pride and doubt disappear, isn't it right? Greed, anger, delusion, pride and doubt exist because the six senses contact their stimuli.

(5) WHAT IS MIND GUIDING? HOW TO GUIDE THE MIND?

Mind guiding has two key components:

a) Guiding the mind to where you need (your mind to inhabit). For instance, you guide the mind toward your aspiration of correctly practicing the True Buddha Dharma, or of becoming vegetarian, or to the thought that eating animal flesh is the act of evil.

b) Guiding the mind to focus on the body, so that the mind is no longer attached to external objects or by haphazard thoughts.

By now, have practitioners seen and understood the truth? Practitioners only need to practice critical thinking on wise attention and the six basic methods fluently, they will then AUTOMATICALLY complete practices mentioned above, don't you think so?

3) Abandoning (familial) fondness

Practicing the True Buddha Dharma requires us to break our fondness and emotional attachments to our family, our sacred and heartfelt love built up and deepened over generations. How can we ever leave those attachments? We can physically leave the family but we may not stop our homesickness and nostalgia. While we make efforts and force ourselves to leave the family, we have obviously suppressed our mind (and the desire of our heart).

(1) The Buddha only gave teachings to people, who were ready to leave their family and without any familial fondness or attachments. The Buddha did not teach people, who were still tightened to their sacred familial responsibilities, the methods for the departer to gain peace of mind throughout his or her journey of Enlightenment and methods for those stay-behind family members to not be saddened by his/her departure.

(2) Arhat Thich Thong Lac continued that tradition by calling practitioners to leave their family to enter a secluded life. He taught that practitioners must not be homesick in order to set both feet on the path of Enlightenment. He

taught that if a practitioner set only one foot on the "Buddhist boat" while the other foot stayed on shore of secular life - a half-hearted voyager, his "boat" would not move, and thus, neither of his pursuits will be fulfilled! Some people may have managed to achieve both but this case is extremely rare. Most people failed at solitary retreat (because of familial fondness). Some postulants strongly opposed Venerable Thong Lac when He prevented them to meet with their wife and children, leading to a confrontation. One postulant even said to the Venerable: "I will be better at Buddhism than you. The postulant later moved to the U.S. to seek social assistance from the State and spent his time - (instead of striving for liberation from suffering and afflictions) - waiting for his day to come, the day he follows his departed ancestors!

(3) Do not worry! With critical thinking on wise attention and the six basic methods,

the practitioner will be able to leave his family in calm, peace and comfort, so that he can set both feet on his Buddhist voyage and proceed directly toward Enlightenment. It is clear! Practitioners should calmly continue their normal activities with their family, society and career. The only difference is that practitioner should nurture and keep in mind the aspiration for his liberation (from the samsara), and should spare some time and space for the practice just like doing a daily exercise. Practitioners should spare a specific time for a quiet practice in a closed-door space. Practitioners should first conduct one-method practice, plus long-distance walking meditation IN ORDER TO KNOW IF YOU CAN TAKE IT OR NOT. If you can, and have become comfortable with those, it's time for you to practice critical thinking & commanding on wise attention, and the six basic methods. When you have become fluent with the initial practices and your mind is imbued with true Buddhist qualities, opportunities will come for you to choose one suitable method and use it as the accoutrement/gear for your voyage to Buddhahood.

It is very clear.

a) For our family members, they have already prepared their mindset for the separation throughout the time that practitioners exercise the Dharma at home. They warmly and comfortably see us off with hopes and expects for our triumphant return. They themselves also wish to be able to practice the Dharma.

b) As for the practitioner, you (also) have well prepared for the separation. You will not be afraid of solitude and you have been familiar with taking only one meal per day. And so you can gracefully step onto your "cruise ship" and start your liberating voyage, for the silken rope of affinities and familial fondness is finally broken, thus, no more feeling of attachments. It makes sense that when a practitioner is comfortable with solitude, your six senses will automatically turn inward and focus on his body. His mind would no longer care for anything else but for himself. Effectively, the practitioner can proceed with his both feet on the quest of liberation as a wholehearted voyager. That aligns with Arhat Thich Thong Lac's expects, doesn't it?

c) Throughout the process, the practitioner must know how to effectively combine the methods of critical thinking on wise attention and the technique of GRADUAL PROGRESSION instructed by Bhiksu Thanh Thien in order to perfect the six basic methods. With these skills handy, the practitioner will be so well equipped for his journey for Enlightenment that there would be no obstacles that he can't surmount.

Now it's very clear, as Bhiksu Thanh Thien has taught practitioners, that the method of critical thinking on wise attention and the six basic methods would effectively help them peacefully separate from FONDNESS, isn't it?

4) Unfollow the subconscious mind

Practitioners must understand that although the SUBCONSCIOUS MIND HARMS OUR LIFE and we want to stay away from its influence, it is not us who abandon the subconscious mind. Instead, it is our heart which MUST abandon the subconscious mind. We ourselves cannot leave the subconscious mind. WHY?

(1) Practitioners should clearly imagine a picture:

a) You are the king.

b) Your body is the royal palace.

c) Standing on your left side is the CONSCIOUS MIND, a loyal servant.

d) Standing on your right side is the SUBCONSCIOUS MIND, a flattering servant.

e) The Heart is the king's most beloved one. The king goes anywhere that the Heart wants. If the king does not satisfy the Heart, it will annoy him until he follows it. The Heart is a child. Even when the body grows old, THE HEART STILL IS a mindless child.

(2) The HEART is influenced by the subconsciousness and consciousness. If the HEART follows the subconsciousness, the king becomes an EVIL PERSON. If the Heart follows consciousness, the king becomes a GOOD PERSON.

(3) An important point: The HEART is like a child; thus it DOES NOT HAVE its own CONSCIOUSNESS. It is easy enough to

understand. If the HEART HAS (its own) CONSCIOUSNESS, we would not need to practice the True Buddha Dharma because sometime in the future the Heart could wake up and disgust pleasures, separate itself from the subconscious mind and follow the conscious mind to enter the states of wholesomeness. We would then automatically achieve Enlightenment, isn't that right? There is no such thing as internal heart or external heart. The Heart is a child. Once it is familiar with chili food, it annoys us when we do not eat chili food. As it is used to eating animal flesh, it irritates us when we practice vegetarianism. Once it gets used to killing people, it would likewise disturb us if we do not kill people. The Heart follows habits built up by the subconscious mind and the conscious mind. It accepts things routinely introduced to the body and the mind. It tends to reject anything FOREIGN (as if our body rejects antigens), regardless they are right or wrong, good or evil.

(4) The problem is that the CONSCIOUS MIND only starts its operation after we past 18 years of age. Only then does the conscious mind starts functioning. Effectively:

a) Right after our birth, the subconscious mind starts operation. As a result, the subconscious mind feeds certain habits to our Heart. The Heart follows the subconscious mind and inhabit unwholesome deeds. Consequently, the king is EVIL PERSON engaging in all sorts of savage and nasty things. Humankind in its early time is more poisonous than snakes and more savage than tigers.

b) The Buddha created a systematic protocol of THE BUDDHA DHARMA PRACTICE for the human to turn themselves into VIRTUOUS BEING. Because the conscious mind operates too weakly, it does not have sufficient power to convince the Heart to live in the states of wholesomeness. Only when the conscious mind is successful in convincing the Heart of wholesomeness, will the king become VIRTUOUS BEING. In order to help the conscious mind to attract the Heart to the realm of wholesomeness, the Buddha created the method of CRITICAL THINKING & COMMANDING ON WISE ATTENTION which is temporarily considered as a rein used for Heart taming.

c) However, if the conscious mind engages the method of critical thinking & commanding on wise attention to pull the HEART to wholesomeness, THE HEART WILL OPPOSE AND RESIST. When we suppress the Heart, the king will not be able to become VIRTUOUS BEING.

d) That's why Bhiksu Thanh Thien shares the technique of GRADUAL PROGRESSION.

The conscious mind would engage the method of critical thinking on wise attention and technique of GRADUAL PROGRESSION in harmony to make the Heart gradually gets used to (following) the conscious mind. When the Heart is familiar with the conscious mind, it will become bored of and then peacefully leave the subconscious mind to stay with the conscious mind. As a result, the king becomes a perfectly virtuous human being.

(5) If the conscious mind deploys the method of critical thinking on wise attention to attract the Heart with TOO MUCH FORCE, the SUBCONSCIOUS MIND will use a similar force to pull the Heart back. Our practices will not succeed then. That's why the technique of GRADUAL PROGRESSION invented by Bhiksu Thanh Thien inspired by Ms. Ut Dieu Quang is truly amazing. It helps the Mind gradually become familiar with consciousness. When the Heart becomes familiar and intimate with the

conscious mind, it will peacefully and willingly inhabit the states of wholesomeness without being pulled back by the subconscious mind. As the result, the king will gracefully become a genuinely virtuous person. Since then, the king will have mastered the (power of the) Heart, brought it to the states of wholesomeness and progressed toward the MEDITATIONAL STATE OF IMPERTURBABILITY. The king can then gently enter meditation and achieve the Threefold Knowledge without difficulties.

(6) In order to help the Heart peacefully and willingly stay with the conscious mind, Bhiksu Thanh Thien teaches practitioners the method of critical thinking on wise attention and the six basic methods. When practitioners skillfully practice the method of critical thinking on wise attention, THE HEART WILL GRACEFULLY leave the subconscious mind and come to stay with the conscious mind. The HEART will then willingly obey

the king's commands to enter the state of imperturbability, so that the king can enter meditation, achieve the Threefold Knowledge and reach Enlightenment to end SUFFERING. The methods taught by Bhiksu Thanh Thien are clearly magnificent, aren't they?

5) When the heart leaves the subconscious mind to enter the states of wholesomeness, what will the subconscious mind do?

(1) The Buddha affirmed that after we die, our subconscious mind would not leave our body immediately. It would leave the body after six days.

(2) Arhat Thich Thong Lac also agreed with this statement. He said: When a practitioner dies, his/her body should be kept for six days so that the subconscious mind could continue its progress of practice (the True Buddha Dharma).

(3) Those who use subconscious mind for their spiritual practices can also feel that (the subconscious mind lingers 6 days after death).

(4) Bhiksu Thanh Thien confirms that when the Heart - or when we wholeheartedly - enters the states of wholesomeness, the subconscious mind returns to the path of righteousness and follows the path. Consequently, many people with good opportunities have achieved Enlightenment right before their death. Some good examples include the BUDDHA's father and some seniors achieved Enlightenment during their moments. That happens because the subconscious mind took over and continued the practice for us.

TABLE OF CONTENTS

VIETNAM LAWYERS ASSOCIATION
HONG DUC PUBLISHING HOUSE
Address: 65 Trang Thi street, Hoan Kiem district, Ha Noi.
Email: nhaxuatbanhongduc@yahoo.com
Tel: 024.3 9260024 Fax: 024.3 9260031

DEALING WITH THE SUBCONSCIOUS MIND

BHIKSU THICH THANH THIEN

Producer
Director
BÙI VIỆT BẮC
Content
Editor-in-chief
LÝ BÁ TOÀN

Editor : PHAN THỊ NGỌC MINH
Cover : SANG LÊ
Presented by : VY LINH

1000 prints, format 13 x 20cm, at Ha Noi Trading Development JSC.
Address: 53, 16 group, Long Bien ward, Long Bien district, Ha Noi.
Publishing plan registration number: 116-2020/CXBIPH/30-02/HĐ
Publication decision number of publishing house: 30/QĐ-NXBHĐ, January 14th 2020.
Printed and submitted for 2020 reference.
International standard book number (ISBN): 978-604-955-658-6